Preface

KT-118-597

This guide to Madeira is one of the new generation of Baedeker guides.

Illustrated throughout in colour, they are designed to meet the needs of the modern traveller. They are quick and easy to consult, with the principal sights described in alphabetical order, and practical details and useful tips shown in the margin. The information is presented in a format that is both attractive and easy to follow.

The subject of this guide is the Portuguese archipelago of Madeira, including the main island of Madeira, the nearby island of Porto Santo to the north-east, as well as the Ilhas Desertas in the south-east of the group of islands.

The guide is in three parts. The first part gives a general account of the country, its topography climate, flora and fauna, population and administration, economy, transport, art and culture, famous people and the history of the island. A brief selection of quotations and some suggested routes lead into the second part, in which the principal places of tourist interest – towns, villages, landscapes – are described. The third part contains a variety of practical information designed to help visitors to find their way about and make the most of their stay. Baedeker Specials deal, among other things, with Madeira wine, Reid's Hotel and the Levadas. Both the sights and the practical information sections are listed in alphabetical order

This road builder allows himself a rest in front of the magnificent scenery of his native island of Madeira

The new Baedeker guides are noted for their concentration on essentials and their convenience of use. They contain numerous specially drawn plans and colour illustrations, and at the end of the book is a large map making it easy to locate the various places described in the "A to Z" section of the guide with the help of the co-ordinates given at the head of each entry.

Contents

Baedeker

MADEIRA

How to use this book

Following the tradition established by Karl Baedeker in 1844, sights of particular interest, outstanding buildings, works of art, etc. as well as good hotels are indicated by one or two stars as follows: especially worth attention ★, outstanding ★★.

To make it easier to locate the various places listed in the "A to Z" section of the Guide, their co-ordinates on the large city map are shown in red at the head of each entry.

Only a selection of hotels, restaurants and shops can be given; no reflection is implied therefore on establishments not included.

In a time of rapid change it is difficult to ensure that all the information given is entirely accurate and up-to-date, and the possibility of error can never be entirely eliminated. Although the publishers can accept no responsibility for inaccuracies and omissions, they are always grateful for corrections and suggestions for improvement.

Baedeker Specials

Bemvindo

"There are practically no public entertainments. There are neither museums nor galleries. The theatre is quite unprepossessing". So wrote the German pathologist Paul Langerhans in 1885 in his "Handbook to Madeira". Langerhans, who had come to the island in the hope of finding a cure for his tuberculosis, was nevertheless able, over 100 years ago, to appreciate Madeira's many benefits, which more than outweighed its lack of cultural attractions. Not only did he eloquently praise the mild salutary climate, but also went into superlatives in describing the magnificent scenery and the islanders' hospitality. And in none of those respects has anything altered today. Moreover, today's visitors can fly to Madeira, instead of having to make the ocean crossing in small rickety boats. Apart from that, however, Madeira has remained what it was in Langerhans' time: one of the most beautiful islands, if not even the most beautiful island, on the continent of Europe and today there is a wide range of entertainments, museums and galleries. What will most strike the visitor, however, is the island's astonishing variety, lying as it does just a few hundred sea miles from the African coast in the middle of the Atlantic Ocean. Virtually no other island can offer such a spectacular and varied landscape of breathtaking proportions in a land area of just 741 sq. km. There are steeply towering rock faces, deep green

Bizarre

formations of lava are found on the coast of Madeira

Madeira wine

has been found to keep for more than 150 years

a Madeira

valleys and surf-tossed coasts. Anyone who has stood high up on the viewing platform above the Curral das Freiras and is not struck dumb with amazement must be a hardened traveller indeed. The "island of eternal spring" is how Madeira is known on account of its mild climate and visitors have always fallen under its spell. Winston Churchill fell so in love with the tiny fishing port of Câmara de Lobos that he kept on returning with his paint-brush and artist's palette.

There is another side to Madeira, however, which has nothing to do with its being a fascinating natural paradise. Its very remoteness

has caused problems for the island. Although Madeira wine may be a world-famous speciality, little is mentioned of the sheer backbreaking toil which is required of those who make a living from growing the vines. And who can blame the island's young people if they choose to live their lives elsewhere, rather than on an island where there is little hope of a worthwhile professional career? After all, the average monthly income is one of the lowest in Europe.

Pirates
attacked the island of Madeira again and again

Those who ponder these unresolved questions of the present, as well as the island's spectacular scenery, will take more away with them than just a memory of the stupendous view down into the Curral das Freiras. At any rate, welcome to Madeira and "Bemvindo"!

National costume
is nowadays seen on Madeira only at festivals

Facts and Figures

General

Madeira –
island of
flowers in the
Atlantic

Madeira has always enjoyed the title "Island of flowers in the Atlantic Ocean" and is a favoured winter destination for tourists from Northern and Central Europe. Its attractions are not just the pleasant climate, which between November and February can boast average temperatures of about 20°C, but also its magnificent scenery and wonderfully luxuriant flowers and plants which bloom all the year round. It is often forgotten, however, that Madeira – like the Portuguese motherland to which the island has for centuries belonged – is one of the least advantaged places in the European Union. Anyone who takes a closer look at the living conditions of the Madeirans will immediately see that despite various initiatives on the part of the European Union, there is an obvious social divide. Visitors to Madeira should be aware of this, even while they enjoy the fascinating diversity of the island.

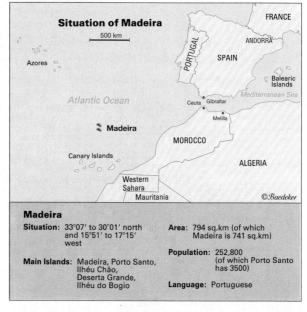

Madeira

Situation: 33°07′ to 30°01′ north and 15°51′ to 17°15′ west

Main Islands: Madeira, Porto Santo, Ilhéu Chão, Deserta Grande, Ilhéu do Bogio

Area: 794 sq.km (of which Madeira is 741 sq.km)

Population: 252,800 (of which Porto Santo has 3500)

Language: Portuguese

Geographical
location

The archipelago of Madeira (in Portuguese: Archipélago da Madeira) lies between 33°7′ and 30°1′N and 15°51′ and 17°15′W in the eastern Atlantic Ocean. It is about 500km from the continent of Africa and some 990km from Lisbon, the Portuguese capital. The Canary Islands are about 445km to the south-west.

◀ *The small fishing town of Camara de Lobos which Winston Churchill, on visiting Madeira, fell in love with*

Madeira is a volcanic island. The fjord-like deep inlets with deep towering rock faces are impressive

When describing the topography of Madeira it is worth recalling the story – albeit of no historical authenticity – of the meeting between Christopher Columbus and Queen Isabella of Spain. When the Queen asked the former to describe the West Indian island of Jamaica, Columbus took a piece of paper, crumpled it up and laid it before the Queen. Columbus also knew Madeira well and who is to say that on another occasion he might not have similarly crumpled up a piece of paper in order to illustrate the topography of Madeira?

Topography and scenery

The archipelago of Madeira consists of the main island Madeira, which rises from a depth of 4000–5000m out of the Atlantic to an average height of over 800m above sea level. With a length of 57km and a maximum width of 22km the main island occupies a land area of 741 sq.km. The archipelago also includes the smaller island of Porto Santo (43km distant; highest point 517m), the three islets of Ilhéu Chão, Deserta Grande and Ilhéu do Bugio, 20km to the south-east and the five uninhabited islands known as the Ilhas Selvagens, about 315km away on the northern edge of the Canaries and with a total area of about 4 sq.km.

All the islands in the Madeiran archipelago are mountainous and, like the Spanish Canary Islands, owe their existence to volcanic activity which occurred in the Mesozoic period, i.e. about 5 to 25 million years ago, and produced a number of extinct craters (lagoas). The subsequent rise of the subsoil by as much as 400m above its original level corresponds to a similar phenomenon on the Canaries. The backbone of the main island of Madeira is a ridge running from east to west, which reaches its highest point with the 1861m high Pico Ruivo (Red Peak) de Santana. This jagged steep crest is similar in shape to the Dolomites. In the west of the island lies the high plateau of Paúl da Serra, while the smaller Santo António da Serra is situated in the east.

On the southern and northern slopes of the central mountain chain are found magnificent high-lying mountain valleys (currais), surrounded by high rock faces. These valleys' outlets to the sea are formed by deeply indented ravines caused by erosion. The ravines on the north coast are especially beautiful and impressive and it is here that it is possible to make out quite clearly the frequent alternation of strata of ash and lava. The coastline of Madeira is steep and rocky; only in a few places, where former flows of lava empty into the sea, are there narrow expanses of beach.

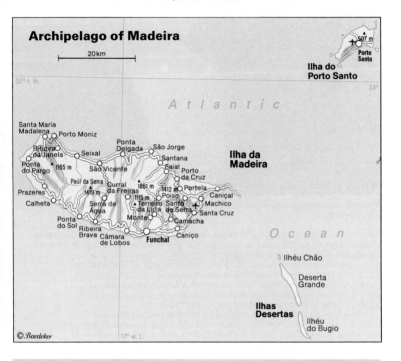

Climate

The island of "eternal spring"

The island of Madeira owes its luxuriant vegetation to an extremely oceanic climate which, by virtue of its situation in the low latitudes, is also warm. In winter low pressure areas from northerly latitudes determine the weather, in the summer months it is dictated by the northeast trade wind. The latter causes big climatic differences between the northern windward side of the island and the southern leeward side. The reason for this is the build-up of cloud caused by moist air masses brought by the north wind, which tend to become trapped, particularly in the morning, by the island's mountain range. Around midday these air masses become warmer, are able to rise, thereby having an impact on the weather on the south side of the island as well.

In simplified terms Madeira can be divided into four climatic zones: the area below 400m which is dry and warm and in summer completely dry and hot; the next zone up, which is more temperate and rainy; a cloudy zone extending from about 100m upwards which has rainfall all the year round; and finally a higher dry zone above the trade wind clouds which occurs above 1400–1500m.

On the north side, where the trade winds meet the mountain slopes, large quantities of rain fall, mainly in the winter months. For example, the village of Santana in the north of the island has an average rainfall of 1314mm per year, with the extremes being November with 215mm and July with only 27mm. In the higher zones there can be 2000mm of rainfall per year, as for example at the pass of Encumeada which has an average of 2675mm. On the south side of the island the average rainfall is usually well below 600mm.

Except in the noticeably dry months of July and August, showers can be expected all over Madeira, with longer periods of rain inland.

Selected Weather Data												
Average	Jan.	Feb.	March	Apr.	May	June	July	Aug.	Sept.	Oct.	Nov.	Dec.
Day temp in °C	19	19	19	20	21	22	24	25	25	24	22	20
Night temp in °C	13	13	14	14	15	18	19	20	19	18	16	14
Sunshine hours per day	5	6	6	7	8	6	8	8	7	7	5	5
Rain days per month	7	6	7	4	2	1	0	1	2	7	7	7
Water temp in °C	15	14	14	15	17	18	21	22	21	19	17	16

Source: German Meteorological Service, Offenbach

Temperatures

The island's location on the same degree of latitude as Cairo is responsible for determining the average temperature. Even in winter the temperature seldom falls below 18°C in the lower-lying areas, while the temperature change at a higher latitude can be considerable. In the highest mountain areas it is quite possible for snow to fall.

There is a significant difference between the south and north sides of the island; whereas the annual average temperature at Funchal is about 18.2°C, on the north (wetter) side at Ponta Delgada it is only 17.4°C. Occasionally hot air masses are brought over by an easterly wind from the Sahara; these winds called the Spanish Leste (east), can sometimes be very unpleasant as, along with the hot Saharan air, they bring desert sand.

Water temperatures

Water temperatures vary between 17°C in March and 20–23°C in high summer (July/August).

Flora and Fauna

Flora

Originally Madeira was covered by dense forest...

When João Gonçalves Zarco and Tristão Vaz Teixeira with their followers discovered Madeira in 1419, they found an island of steep and rough terrain, covered by thick forest – hence the island's name ("Madeira" is Portuguese for "wood").

It was not least the obvious intractability of the island's terrain which caused the discoverers first of all to settle on the more easily

The flora in Madeira is unusually varied

accessible neighbouring island of Porto Santo and use the latter as a base from which to open up and explore the main island. It took several centuries to make the island suitable for cultivation, the most appropriate method for the early Portuguese settlers being to clear away the forests by burning.

According to contemporary documents these burnings took place over a period of at least seven years, and when the fires were finally extinguished, only a tiny part was left of the original primeval forest which had existed for thousands of years. The clearances were followed by the establishment of an irrigation system (the levadas), which was constructed using slaves brought over from the African coast. These developments may have made Madeira suitable for economic exploitation, but at the same time they profoundly altered the original landscape.

...only traces remain of the lauraceous woods

Only traces remain of the original lauraceous woods, which were widespread during the Mesozoic period, not just on Madeira and other Atlantic islands, such as the Canaries, Azores and Cape Verde Islands, but also all over the Mediterranean region. Today these surviving pockets of woodland are the nucleus of Madeira's nature preservation area. There are still substantial stocks of Madeiran laurel (*Laurus indicus*), (*Oreodaphne foetens*) and Canarian laurel (*Laurus azorica*). At heights of over 1000m examples of endemic flora have been preserved: juniper (*Juniperus cedrus*), the wild oil-tree (*Olea maderensis*), and at heights over 1500m tree heath (*Erica scoparia*) and shield fern (*Polystichum falcinellum*).

The dragon tree (*Dracaena draco*), probably the most striking of all the indigenous plants, has largely disappeared on account of the many uses its wood could be put to, and is only to be found in a few places, although all the more impressive because of its paucity.

Exotic plants such as orchids bloom in profusion

Recently, however, it is being increasingly grown as an ornamental addition to parks and gardens.

Eucalyptus woods have been established above 800m as a predominant variety as a result of reafforestation. Both types of tree, *Eucalyptus globulus* and *Eucaluptus ficifolia*, originally came from Australasia and were not brought over to Europe until this century. As a fast-growing wood with many varied uses eucalyptus is much prized. The characteristic aroma of the eucalyptus woods will delight the rambler and a eucalyptus branch in the back of the car can afford similar pleasure to the motorist. Sweets with an excellent flavour are manufactured on Madeira from the ethereal oils of the eucalyptus tree.

A result of reafforestation: eucalyptus woods

Fennel (*Foeniculum vulgare*) was widespread on Madeira at the time of the island's discovery. Today it is still used in the manufacture of sweets, while the town of Funchal owes its name to the plant. Funchal's wide bay, shaped like a Greek amphitheatre, was where Portuguese seafarers landed in the 15th c. and the newcomers were so enchanted by the scent of fennel which they found there that they named the town they built after it.

Fennel gave Funchal its name

Today the vegetation on Madeira, the "Flower of the Ocean" (Portuguese "Flor do Océano"), is characterized by a wealth of magnificent plants, both decorative and functional, which come from all corners of the earth and grow in almost tropical luxuriance, on account of the mild climate, the plentiful winter rains and the artificial watering system provided by the levadas, which channel spring water from the mountains, partly underground through tunnels (furados), to the fields and gardens along the coast. Besides pines and European deciduous trees, countless evergreen trees and shrubs of subtropical

Thanks to the mild climate, Madeira blooms with tropical luxuriance

15

and tropical origin flourish here, including palms, araucaria, hickory, cork-oaks, camphor and fig trees, papaya, palm lilies, yuccas, medlars, mimosa, eucalyptus, bamboo, papyrus reeds, tree ferns and agaves.

The roadsides are often lined with commercially grown, blue-flowered hortensias (*Hydrangea macrophylla*) and the belladonna lily (*Brunsvigia rosea*), which originally came from South Africa.

A wide variety of orchids are grown in commercial orchid gardens, although visiting them can be rather disappointing because the flowering period of individual types varies considerably and the plants are rather unprepossessing when not in bloom. As a lasting and easily cared for souvenir, however, orchids are very popular.

The gardens of Funchal, most of which are surrounded by high walls, delight the visitor in winter and even more so in spring, with their varied array of flowers: roses, camellias, rhododendrons, azaleas, pelargoniums, begonias, bignonias (including *Jacaranda cuspidifolia*), daturas, bougainvilleas, glyzinias and many more. The Christmas Star (*Euphorbia pulcherrima*), which originally came from Mexico, grows into tall shrubs on Madeira. The strelitzia (*Strelitzia reginae*), introduced about 200 years ago from South Africa, is to be found in almost every garden and is also grown on a large scale for export. Its striking flowers, resembling a bird's head, are, if carefully packed, another popular souvenir.

Madeira is also rich in fruit and vegetables

The wealth of plant life on Madeira is no less evident on a visit to the market. As cultivation is possible all the year round, and growers normally aim to bring in several harvests during the course of the year, the island can be considered completely self-sufficient in fruit and vegetables, to the extent that a substantial part of agricultural production is destined for export. Fruit and vegetables are usually only imported when there is a need to balance supply and demand.

The most important commercially grown products are grapes and bananas. With its excellent volcanic soil, low in lime, its adequate rainfall and large amounts of sunshine, the island is particularly suited to the growing of vines (see Baedeker Special).

Bananas are grown along the southern coast (varieties include *Musa acuminata* and *Musa paradisiaca* and can be harvested all the year round. The smaller and less succulent looking types are in general sweeter and more flavoursome than the larger varieties. One of Madeira's culinary specialities is to serve fish with a grilled banana. Sugar cane, which was once of considerable commercial importance, is today only grown for the production of Madeira's version of rum, known as "aguardente". Clumps of wild sugar cane can be found all over the island.

Fauna

Madeira's animal kingdom is very limited

In contrast to the wealth of Madeira's flora, its fauna is very limited. As with the developmental history of any small isolated biosphere without contact with other faunas, only a very small number of endemic species were able to evolve and survive on Madeira. Unlike plants, which can propagate by means of seeds carried by the wind, animals are dependent on their own strength if they are to swim or fly across the sea to an island such as Madeira.

Thus the largest number of indigenous species is to be found among insects, many of which, by process of adaptation, have lost their ability to fly. Endemic is the poisonous wolf spider (*Geolycosa ingens*), which is only to be found on Deserta Grande.

The only reptiles are frogs and the Madeiran lizard, which causes severe damage in both gardens and farms and is therefore treated as a pest by farmers. Wild and domestic animals such as cows, horses,

An attractive pond at Ribeiro Frio where rainbow trout are bred

donkeys, goats, sheep, pigs, hedgehogs and rabbits reached the island after its discovery by man, along with pests such as rats and mice. The only indigenous mammal is the bat.

Another of man's imports is the rainbow trout, which is farmed at Ribeiro Frio, the fish subsequently being released into mountain streams for the benefit of sporting anglers.

There is a rich variety of bird life. Some 200 types of bird are resident here or come to lay their eggs, including birds of prey such as buzzards and falcons, and also canaries (*Serinus canaris*), Madeira ring-doves (*Columba trocaz*) and the petrel (*Thalassidroma bulwerii*).

The waters around Madeira do not contain large stocks of fish, owing to their great depth. There is no suitable habitat for those creatures which in other parts of the world can exist in salt-water or shallow sea water, such as mussels, crabs and flat fish. Apart from the espada (see below), the fish which can be caught in the waters around Madeira include tuna, rosefish and squid. Whaling, which used to be carried out around Caniçal, was discontinued in 1981. However, the heyday of Madeira's whaling industry is commemorated by a small museum at Caniçal which has various exhibits and documents from the period.

Marine life

The sea around Ponta do Garajau has been turned into a conservation area, the Reserva Natural Parcial do Garajau, in order to protect marine flora and fauna, and the level of fishing permitted has been drastically reduced. This superb underwater landscape can be observed either using diving equipment or from a mini-submarine.

Monk seals (*Monachinae*), which were once common around the Canary Islands and in the Mediterranean, also used to inhabit the bay of Câmara de Lobos in vast numbers, giving the bay its name (lobo = wolf), but they have been practically wiped out. Only around the Ilhas Desertas can a dozen or more still be found and these are strictly protected. For that reason it is not permitted to land on the islands.

scabbard fish , *a speciality of Madeira on sale in the Mercado dos Lavradores*

Espada
(Scabbard fish)

The most important edible fish, and to some extent a Madeiran speciality, is the espada or scabbard fish (*Espada preta*), which is only to be found around Madeira and in Japan. Black and shaped like an eel, it is a deep-sea fish which belongs to the *Trichiuridae* group and can be as much as 2m long. As it is thought to live at depths of more than 800m (hence its exaggeratedly large eyes) and only comes any higher at night, fishing lines up to 2000m in length are needed to catch it.

An old wives' tale, which once used to have currency, maintained that the espada was really mother-of-pearl colour and only turned black when it came into contact with air. In fact there are two varieties – a light one and a dark one. What is true, however, is that the espada has firm tasty flesh and is never absent from menus on Madeira.

Population and Administration

Area and
population

The main island of Madeira has an area of 741 sq.km. and the population according to official figures is about 300,000. If the areas of the neighbouring island of Porto Santo, the (uninhabited) Ilhas Desertas and the distant Ilhas Selvagens (which count as part of the archipelago) are also taken into account, the total land area is 794 sq.km.

Demographic
history

Henry the Navigator was given the archipelago of Madeira by the Portuguese King Duarte I in 1433 as a feudal payment and immediately began enlisting the services of Portuguese settlers. In addition, during several voyages along the African coast, he traded in slaves as well as gold and spices. These slaves were brought over to Madeira in the first place to help in the production of sugar cane – one of the most lucrative trades in the island's economic history. Today descendants of the original slaves still live on the island, although they have long since been assimilated and are now Portuguese citizens.

The main characteristic of Madeiran population structure is the extended family. Families, especially in the more rural areas, often consist of six or more children. At the same time, however, population growth as a whole is stagnating, just as it is in the rest of Portugal, and since 1981 the number of births has not exceeded the number of deaths.

People of Madeira: an old woman, a young student and a young man in a typical bobble cap

The average density of population of Madeira is about 380 people per sq.km., although this figure does not reveal anything about the actual distribution of population. The south coast of Madeira, which enjoys the best climatic conditions, is also much more heavily populated than the rest of the island, with close on two fifths of the total population living in Funchal, Madeira's only real town. Thus the north of the island is quite sparsely populated, whereas Funchal and the villages scattered around it have a population of some 108,000. This is not least accounted for by the fact that Funchal is the centre of the Madeiran tourist industry and employment opportunities are better here than in other parts of the island.

Population distribution

Despite the fact that for many years now the number of tourists visiting the islands has been constantly increasing, the opportunities of finding a good job, even for young people with high-level qualifications, have continued to be very scarce. This harsh fact is evidenced by the very high number of Madeirans who choose to leave the island. Many young people, when they have finished their schooling, go to the Portuguese mainland, or on to other countries in Western Europe. Overseas, other popular destinations include the Portuguese and Spanish speaking countries of Brazil and Venezuela, the United States of America and Canada.

The problem of emigration

As in the rest of Portugal, by far the largest proportion of the population, some 94.5%, count themselves as Roman Catholics, although it is a significant fact that the Catholic church has forfeited a considerable part of its former influence over Madeirans, especially among the young people living in and around Funchal. Away from the capital, however, the traditional religious domination of village life still exists and religious processions are among the high points of the yearly calendar.

Religion

Economy

Administration

Since 1974, when what has come to be known as Portugal's Carnation Revolution took place, Madeira has enjoyed a high degree of autonomy. even though the formal statute of autonomy failed to be passed in 1980, either by the Portuguese constitutional commission or by the revolutionary council in power at that time. Madeira has always been and continues to be represented by the motherland of Portugal in all external affairs. By tacitly granting internal autonomy to the islands in the 1970s, the government in Lisbon in effect forestalled the objectives of a militant anticommunist separatist group, known as FLAMA (Frente de Libertação da Madeira), which had been fighting for complete independence from Portugal. The group lost its influence, which at times had been considerable, when the bloodless coup (hence called the 'Carnation Revolution') of April 1974 finally ended the era of the Portuguese dictator António de Oliveira Salazar (1889–1970).

Flag of Madeira

Funchal – capital of Madeira

Funchal, the only large town on Madeira, is the seat of administration, and of the president and legislature. Madeira's government consists of a president, a vice-president and six regional secretaries; political decisions are made by a regional parliament of 55 members.

Since 1976 the Social Democratic Party (PSD) has been uninterruptedly in power. However, the PSD is by European standards relatively right-wing in complexion.

Administrative structure

The island of Madeira is divided into eleven districts (concelhos) and each of these comprises about 50 parishes (freguesias). The neighbouring island of Porto Santo counts as a separate concelho and enjoys a certain independence. The PSD also enjoys by far the greatest political support of all the parties at local level.

Economy

Madeira's greatest problem is its topography

Madeira's economic development has always suffered from the fact that only about a third of the island's surface area is cultivable and in order to make even this third usable it was necessary for the first settlers to carry out wholesale forest burning during the 15th and 16th c. In doing this they sacrificed virtually the whole of the island's primeval forest, which had existed for thousands of years.

The landscape of Madeira, particularly as it greets the observer looking at it today from the sea, is the result of centuries of human toil. Terraces (polos) were levelled out of the mountainsides in order to be suitable for agricultural use and before that an elaborate and extensive system of irrigation channels, known as levadas, had been established. These brought water from the wet northern side of the island to those areas which were dryer, but much better suited to farming. The first of these levadas were used to irrigate fields of sugar cane and to work mills. They are thought to have been built by Moorish slaves who were brought over to Madeira from North Africa. By far the largest part of the present-day network of levadas was actually not built until the turn of the century (see Baedeker Special pp.106–107).

Today, financial help from the European Union is playing an increasingly important part in building up and strengthening Madeira's economy. At considerable cost the island's transport network has been extended and modernised.

The network of levadas, which today extends for some 2150km, is the most important prerequisite for high levels of agricultural production on Madeira. On the north coast, and more especially on the south coast, sugar cane has been grown since 1452 and until well into the 19th c. was the most important component of the island's economy (see Baedeker Special, p.22). Sugar from Madeira was much prized all over Europe and could command a correspondingly high price. It was only when the discovery was made that sugar was not only obtainable from sugar cane but could also be extracted from sugar beet that Madeiran sugar quickly lost its importance. As, over the years, the sugar cane had robbed the soil of its essential goodness, most of the fields were unable to be cultivated again for a long time. Today only very small amounts of sugar cane are grown and are mainly used in the production of 'aguardente', a local spirit.

Banana plants are probably among the most delicate and labour-intensive of agricultural crops. It is all the more surprising, then, that on an island like Madeira, which has little or no protection from the elements, almost every square inch of land is used to grow banana plants. In some places, for example in the west of the island, it is even the case that a disproportionately high level of outlay is incurred in order to protect the plants from the effects of the weather.

Yet this impression is only half correct. Since the introduction to the island at the beginning of the last century of the relatively robust Dwarf Cavendish banana, which originated in South China, the fruit has been grown on large plantations and banana exports have been a far from insignificant factor in the economy.

Banana growing enjoyed its heyday on Madeira in the 1920s. British businessmen living on the island ensured that production increased

Funchal harbour: a well-known transshipment port for bananas as well as a port of call for cruise ships

Sugar for the Court of the Tsar

A visit to the small, rather run-down factory at Porto da Cruz is a "must" on any sightseeing tour through the eastern part of Madeira. At harvest time cut sugar cane will be piled up several metres high outside the factory gate, and while workers haul the cane bundles into the half-dark of the building, lorries keep returning with more. Inside the din is tremendous, hissing white steam pushes its way out of copper valves, leather drive-belts rattle away. In the sugar cane factory at Porto da Cruz, one of the last on Madeira, the visitor has

Sugar, along with Madeira wine, was for centuries the island's most important agricultural export. Madeira sugar was even used at the court of the Tsar of Russia, while the princely houses of Europe are among the commodity's most important customers. However, sugar derived from cane was eclipsed as a commodity back in the 18th c. when the Berlin chemist Andreas Sigismund Marggraf made the discovery in 1747 that sugar not only could be produced from sugar cane, but also from sugar beet. Industrial

Aguardente being distilled in Porto da Cruz

the feeling of being transported back into the early age of industrialisation. The machines, which date back to the 1920s, are driven by steam, and in them the sugar cane is stripped, ground and pressed, and the sugar juice purified and later evaporated. After various other processing stages, the raw sugar is finally washed once more, in order to remove any impure coating from the surface of the sugar crystals, and pure white sugar remains.

production of the latter was developed by Franz Carl Achard in 1801 and sugar from Madeira, which had always commanded a high price, very quickly lost its importance. Today there are still a few sugar cane plantations on Madeira, but the sugar is used almost exclusively in the production of the spirit "aguardente". A visit to Porto da Cruz would not be complete without a sip of this "firewater" straight from the distillery.

rapidly in the space of just a few years. Since the fruits are so delicate, they are harvested while still green – as is common practice everywhere – and are ripened while being transported to their various destinations. The need for transportation to be as quick as possible was the most important reason why for many years mainland Portugal was the main market for Madeiran bananas.

Today banana plants occupy about a fifth of Madeira's agricultural land, while the farmers themselves have formed co-operatives in order to secure better markets for their produce. As the quality of the fruit is not especially high, many of the more prestigious markets are out of reach for the Madeirans. It was only as a result of European internal market regulations that import restrictions were imposed on bananas from Caribbean and Latin American countries. In addition there are EU subsidies to protect bananas of lesser quality.

Of all Madeira's agricultural products the vine has the longest tradition. Very soon after the island had been discovered and the first settlers moved in, it was recognised that the island's lava soils were extraordinarily fertile. The fire clearances which were carried out in order to make the island cultivable also brought a further enrichment of the soil through the ashes they produced.

Wine production

As in northern Portugal vines are grown on frames, which has the advantage that the ground underneath can be used for other crops, e.g. sweet potatoes and vegetables.

As Madeira wine would naturally possess a slightly acid taste, it undergoes a highly unusual process: over a period of four or five months it is heated to a temperature of up to 50°C in special wooden casks (estufas), which gives it its characteristic exquisite flavour. Before that a small amount of brandy is added to the young wine in order to halt the fermentation process (see Baedeker Special, pp.144–146).

Vines on Madeira are grown on frames as in northern Portugal

Typical of the agriculture on Madeira are the little flat parcels of land under cultivation

This also has the effect that the wine keeps significantly longer than other types; there are reports of bottles being opened after over 100 years and their contents displaying a real intensity, depth and freshness. When talking of Madeira wine, the adage is certainly true: "the older the better": even wines 20 or 30 years old are still a long way from attaining their maturity, although equally there are also wines which it is recommended be drunk at the tender age of 10 or 15 years.

Madeira wine is always blended according to the traditional Solera principles developed in the Spanish city of Jérez. The aim of this method, which needless to say is a closely guarded secret of every wine dealer in Madeira, is to maintain an absolutely consistent level of quality. The finest Madeira wines are reckoned to be the "reserve" wines, which may only be made using grapes from a single harvest.

Animal husbandry

Only a small area of Madeira is suited to rearing livestock, including the plateau of Paúl da Serra, on which there are a few herds of sheep and goats, mostly living wild. The number of actual sheep on Madeira is estimated at about 10,000, and the number of goats about 12,000. The wool from the sheep tends to produce a coarse variety when spun, but a joint of roast goat meat is a popular feast-day meal.

Characteristic features of the landscape are "palheiros" – tiny stalls, roughly put together, in which cows can be kept. The reason that the cows are very seldom seen is that they spend the greater part of their lives in these stalls and only come out into daylight for the odd hour. Pigs have been kept only in the last few years and probably as a result of increased tourism.

Industry

Industry is of no importance on Madeira, not least because the topographical conditions do not facilitate the setting-up of larger produc-

The Madeira Carlton Hotel – one of the many luxury hotels on the island

tion sites. There are a few smaller businesses around the capital Funchal, but these almost exclusively produce goods for domestic use, not for export.

Madeira has been a popular tourist destination since the 18th c. Its mild oceanic climate did not just attract the usual holidaymakers from Great Britain and other European countries, but also people with lung diseases and gout sufferers who believed they would find a cure for their ailments here. Round about the middle of the 18th c. these visitors were joined in large numbers by members of the courts of kings and princes, and the moneyed aristocracy did not stay away either. Eventually it became fashionable to choose to holiday in Madeira during the damp and cold winters of northern Europe. The first hotels on Madeira, including the celebrated Reid's Hotel (see Baedeker Special, pp.84–85), were already established by the end of the last century. One drawback to Madeira's further development as a tourist destination was certainly the tedious and costly sea crossing. In 1921 a seaplane landed in Funchal Bay for the first time; the service was discontinued again, however, in 1958 after two spectacular fatal crashes. After that Madeira had to wait until 1964 to be given its own airport and have proper air services.

Tourism

The opening of Santa Catarina Airport, situated about 18km east of Funchal, was an absolute prerequisite for any further tourist development on the island. Since then the number of hotel beds has multiplied many times; at the present time there are some 17,000 beds in 118 hotels and numerous small country inns. A further, albeit modest, addition to the island's accommodation capacity is planned for the year 2000, with the rural areas outside Funchal being particularly targeted for development. The airport itself is also being extended at the present time, so that it can accept larger aircraft.

25

Transpor

Transport

The individual
traveller – as
opposed to mass
tourism

If the regional government has its way, the trend will be towards accommodating the individual traveller, rather than following the route of mass tourism. An extension of conference and convention facilities should make Madeira a preferred venue for such events. In 1996 a large trade fair and conference centre (5000sq.m. floor area) was opened in Funchal.

Today tourism is a linchpin of the Madeiran economy, with around 500,000 visitors coming to the island each year. About 5000 people are employed in the hotel industry, with another 15,000 jobs being directly dependent on tourism. The hotel industry alone contributes about 10% of Madeira's gross national product.

Transport

For centuries
Madeira
possessed
the simplest of
road networks . . .

Madeira's topography has always been the single most important obstacle to the development of a modern transport system. For centuries men had to carry heavy loads unaided. In order to overcome often considerable differences in altitude, a network of very simple cobbled tracks was laid, with narrow stone bridges crossing the ravines. There are still many houses today, situated in the more remote parts of the island, which have no vehicular access. One consequence of this is that farmers often have to carry their produce on foot over sometimes considerable distances to the nearest road from where it can be collected and taken by goods vehicle to market or to a bulk purchaser.

In the last few years, however, Madeira has seen a marked improvement in its road network. Thanks in no small part to financial subsidies from the European Union, many double-track highways have been built, with the result that even the remotest parts of the island are now relatively accessible.

. . . along with
some highly
original methods
of transport

Madeira's characteristic system of roads and tracks also led to some highly idiosyncratic methods of transport in the 17th and 18th c. The "rede" was the name given to a hammock attached to one or two poles which was not just used by the better-off Madeirans to get about. The particularly adventurous even had themselves carried up to the top of Pico Ruivo, Madeira's highest mountain, in just such a hammock.

Another method of transport was the palanquin, a kind of litter. It was not only used to transport people, but also goods of all kinds, and consisted of a board surrounded by wooden, or sometimes iron, rails. The palanquin was carried by two "portadores" – men who were strong, and sure on their feet and not inclined to vertigo!

Finally mention must be made of the "carro de bois", a kind of sled pulled by two oxen which was invented by the Englishman Major Buckley in 1848. In comparison with the aforementioned methods of transport this offered considerably more comfort; members of genteel society would have their carro de bois shrouded in fine cloths which offered the occupant protection from the vagaries of the weather.

Another reminder of an age long past is the basket-sled, a method of transport still in use today for covering the distance of 4.8km from Monte to Funchal. Although these sleds are now only used by tourists, there was once a time when they represented a highly practical mode of transport.

The geological form of Madeira is one of the main obstacles ▶
to road development

The "rede": a hammock slung on one or two poles was a favourite method of transport

Until 1943 Madeira even had a railway, which as early as 1893 was installed as a rack-railway between Funchal and Monte. After a spectacular steam-boiler explosion in 1930 the number of passengers dropped dramatically and in 1943 the service was discontinued. Only the old station and a few bridge arches provide a mute testimony to this technological tour de force which managed to surmount an incredible 917m altitude difference.

Public transport has been greatly improved in the last few years

The improvement in transport connections on Madeira is most clearly evident in public transport. A comprehensive network of bus connections makes it possible to get to almost anywhere on the island quickly and comfortably. In the capital Funchal there is a very reliable bus service served by modern vehicles.

Plenty of traffic, but only narrow roads

The high number of private cars being registered in the last few years is becoming very noticeable, especially in Funchal. As the road network is only adequate for much smaller numbers of vehicles, it is inevitable that there are traffic problems some of the time.

Until the road network outside Funchal is improved and extended, allowances will continue to have to be made for the indifferent quality of the existing roads. They are often so narrow that when two vehicles are approaching one another from opposite directions, one of them will have to take refuge in one of the passing places provided in order that the other can pass. At the entrances to tunnels, of which there are many, it is all too likely that water flowing down will have caused a sudden deterioration in the road surface.

Road closures as a result of minor or more serious falls of rocks and stones are also a daily occurrence. Any signs giving advance warning of this sort of disturbance should always be treated seriously.

Santa Catarina, Madeira's only airport, is situated some 18km east of Funchal. On account of its position by a steep mountainside and the very unpredictable fall winds it is considered one of the most difficult airports in Europe for planes to land at. Work to lengthen both the take-off and landing strips, which at present are only 1800m long, coupled with a slight directional rotation, was completed in 1997 and should ease the difficulties experienced by pilots.

Santa Catarina is the name of the only airport

On Porto Santo, the landing strip belonging to the NATO air-base is used for civil flights as well, although only local flights using propeller and turboprop aircraft are allowed.

Santa Catarina Airport has one of the most difficult approaches of any European airport

History

About 20 million years ago: Madeira comes into being

As a consequence of intensive tectonic activity and volcanic eruptions under the sea, there is a piling-up of lava material in the Atlantic Ocean during the Mesozoic period (about 5–25 million years ago). The seabed rises to as much as 400m above its original level. Several million years later the final volcanos become extinct and plants and trees begin to grow on the fertile layer of lava.

The first discovery of Madeira

The Phoenicians were skilled and experienced seafarers and it is possible that they were the first people to discover the island of Madeira. About 2600 years ago they sailed through the Straits of Gibraltar and then along the West African coast. Here they set up trading settlements, but whether they actually set up a similar one on Madeira has not been recorded. At the time of King Juba II of Mauretania (1 B.C.), however, the islands had acquired the name Insulae Purpurariae, on account of the purple dyeing which was carried on there.

About 600 B.C.: Did the Phoenicians come to Madeira?

The archipelago of Madeira was first shown on a Florentine sea chart which appeared under the title "Parte dell'Africa tratta dalla Carta V. del Portulano". Madeira bore the name "Isla de Iolegname", which was perhaps a corruption of the Arabic word "el agham" which roughly means "wood". The neighbouring island of Porto Santo is also shown, with the name "Porto Séo".

14th c.: Madeira = island of wood

Fabulous treasures of gold and spices and the availability of slaves lured European ship crews to the Atlantic coast of Africa. Henry the Navigator set off from Lagos in about 1420 and sailed southwards along the African coast in order to trade in slaves and African gold-dust. The slaves were particularly needed on Madeira to help develop the island's nascent economy. As early as 1419 the Portuguese sailor João Gonçalves Zarco reached the island of Madeira which he described in his ship's log as "uninhabited and covered by dense forest". So it was that the island was given its name – a name which holds good even today – Ilha da Madeira – island of wood. Nevertheless Zarco and his men lacked the courage to set foot on the island and he retreated to Porto Santo where he set up camp and stared distrustfully across at it. What he found particularly strange were the at times highly dramatic cloud formations over the island (he even thought it might possibly be a direct entrance to hell) and it was only after several weeks spent gazing across that he plucked up the courage to make the crossing.

15th c.: The Europeans explore the African continent

The colonisation of Madeira occurred during the course of a massive migratory movement which took place from Spain and Portugal in the late Middle Ages. The Portuguese were always dependent on the import of foodstuffs, in particular grain, and it was this imperative which led to the economic exploitation of Madeira, although the cultivation of wheat and barley was only of importance in the very early years. By 1460 cereals had been replaced as the main crop by sugar cane, which had reached the Mediterranean lands from India via

◄ *The square in front of Funchal Town Hall: a beautiful example of the art of paving*

Egypt. It had quickly been realised that the sugar trade was highly profitable, even taking into account the considerable initial capital outlay. Soon Madeira was famous throughout the western world for the extraordinary quality of its sugar. Merchants even came out from Italy to settle on Madeira and make money out of sugar. Vine-growing also enjoyed a rapid upsurge.

1440–97:
Madeira is
split in two

In 1440 Machico was declared the capital of the eastern part of the island and put under the control of Tristão Vaz Teixeira; four years later Bartolomeu Perestrelo was given the neighbouring island of Porto Santo. The western part of the island of Madeira was finally given to João Gonçalves Zarco in 1450. King Henry the Navigator gave all three the right to demand feudal payments but with the condition that a portion of their income from these should come to him.

It is thought that Christopher Columbus (see Famous People) lived on Porto Santo from 1479. It was here that he is supposed to have made the first nautical calculations which led to the discovery of America in 1492. The division of Madeira into two parts came to an end in 1497, however, when King Manuel I included the island in

Merchant ships in Funchal Bay

his kingdom and named Funchal as the only capital. In 1508 Funchal was given a town charter, and with it came the right to have its own municipal coat of arms. This depicted five sugar loaves, thereby emphasising Madeira's importance as a supplier of sugar. By 1514 Funchal already had more than 5000 inhabitants, a not inconsiderable proportion of whom, however, were enslaved people, mainly of African origin.

Merchant vessels which arrived at Madeira were continually being set upon by pirates, who also tried to land on the island. In order to protect Funchal, King Manuel I had the fortress of São Lourenço built and on both Madeira and Porto Santo look-out posts were installed, which were manned continuously. These sentries had the job of lighting enormous piles of wood at the approach of any pirate ship, thereby warning the populace of the imminent danger. In 1516 Funchal was finally consecrated as a cathedral see and a bishop was ordained. As thanks Pope Leo X was given a replica of St Peter's Church in Rome made out of sugar. In 1566 French freebooters succeeded in carrying out an attack on Funchal. Before help could arrive from the Portuguese mainland all the churches had been plundered.

Constant threat from pirates; Funchal becomes a cathedral see

When Portugal lost its independence from Spain after the death of Henry II, Madeira also became Spanish. But that was not sufficient to protect the inhabitants from the ever increasing threat of pirate raids: in 1620 the English buccaneer John Ward attacked Funchal, took 1200 men, women and children prisoner, deported them to Tunisia and sold them there as slaves.

English merchants come to Madeira

17th c.: Commercial zenith

During the 17th c. the first English merchants settled on the island; they very quickly realised the value of Madeira wine as a profitable trade commodity. Even after Portugal recovered her independence in 1668, the Anglo-Saxon world remained Madeira's chief trading partner, with sugar and wine being the most important commodities.

1801: Madeira is occupied

The Napoleonic Wars even cast their shadow on Madeira. English troops landed on the island and set up a base. Six years later they declared a state of occupation on Madeira – a situation which admittedly only lasted seven years. However, even after the withdrawal of the English forces many Britons remained on Madeira, some of whom left the army and set themselves up as merchants.

1852: Mildew destroys the vines

In 1852 the wine-growing industry on Madeira faced a severe crisis when mildew and then later phylloxera destroyed a large part of the vines. It took many years before grapes were able to grow again on the new vines. Many poor people had no alternative but to emigrate, while others tried their luck at basket-making, a flourishing branch of the Madeiran economy. In addition, the introduction of new embroidery patterns and techniques by the Englishwoman Elizabeth Phelps gave a small but lasting boost to the economy.

The first visitors had also started to come to the island, attracted by its equable and pleasant climate. The world-famous Reid's Hotel was opened in 1891 and its guests soon included crowned – and uncrowned – heads from the whole of Europe. At first visitors had to travel by ship, but latterly, from 1947, they have been able to arrive by plane, as a regular service between London and Funchal came into operation.

From the turn of the century to the present day

1916: German U-boats outside Funchal

After the Portuguese government at England's insistence had confiscated all German possessions as well as a number of ships, German U-boats turned up without warning outside Funchal during the First World War. They not only sank the French merchant ship "Surprise", but also bombarded the town, destroying several buildings. During a rogation procession the people of Madeira vowed to erect a statue of the Madonna at the end of the war. This was financed from all over the world (even the Austrian empress is said to have contributed) and it was erected above Monte in 1927.

The era of Salazar's dictatorship

The era of the dictator António de Oliveira Salazar began with a coup d'état on May 28th 1926. This learned economist founded the "União Nacional" in 1930 and decreed that it should be the country's only political party. On Madeira there were protests against the centralist government in Lisbon and in 1931 there were even violent disturbances which had to be put down with force.

The Second World War passed Madeira by, not least because Portugal declared herself neutral in the conflict. On May 6th 1943 the government in Lisbon broke off diplomatic relations with Germany and handed over military bases on the Azores to the English in 1943 and one year later to the Americans.

The opening of the new airport of Santa Catarina east of Funchal in 1964 made Madeira an easily accessible destination from almost anywhere in Europe. Up until this time visitors had had to land at the NATO airport on Porto Santo and then face a sea-crossing of several hours. As a consequence of the new transport links the tourist industry on Madeira enjoyed a growth rate well into double figures. At the same time, however, the government reaffirmed its commitment that the island should continue to cater mainly for individual travellers.

1964: Madeira gets its own airport

After various attempted coups from groups committed to democracy, Salazar's reign came to an end with his resignation in 1968. One of his followers, Marcelo José das Neves Alves Caetano, took power on an interim basis and then in 1974 democracy prevailed in Portugal with the "Carnation Revolution": members of the military seized power in a largely bloodless coup and instigated a socialist-oriented set of reforms.

1974: Democrats take over the government

In common with Portugal's other overseas colonies, Madeira was given a large measure of autonomy in 1976. The archipelago was renamed the "Região Autónoma da Madeira" (autonomous region of Madeira). Dr Alberto João Jardim, a well-liked politician, was the victor in the first elections and took over the reins of government, which he still holds. Jardim's party, the PSD, gained the largest number of seats in the regional parliament while Jardim has shown himself to be a staunch advocate of maintaining the status quo with regard to Madeira's political subordination to Portugal.

Madeira remains Portuguese, but . . .

The introduction of the European internal market has brought Portugal, and therefore Madeira, substantial economic assistance from the European Union. This influx of funds is directed primarily to the opening up of the island through new technological improvements in the transport network, the deficiencies of which had always acted as a brake to the island's economic development.

1993: The European internal market is introduced

Famous People

Listed below in alphabetical order are historical figures who were born, spent time, worked or died in Madeira and attained international recognition.

John Blandy
(1783–1855)
merchant

The Briton John Blandy was born in Dorchester in 1783 and came to Madeira for the first time in 1807 as quartermaster for the British garrison. He fell in love with the island and four years later, after leaving military service, he settled on the island for good. Blandy purchased the house at 8, Rua de São Francisco and founded a business dealing in Madeira wine. "Blandy's Madeira Wine Company" became well-known all over Europe and had successful branches not just in England, but also in Lisbon and later on Gran Canaria. The method by which Blandy laid the foundation for his later wealth was simple and yet logical: the ships which docked at Madeira and delivered goods such as coal to the island, did not, as they might have done, travel back empty to their port of departure, but instead carried wine at highly advantageous freight prices. John Blandy's son, Charles Ridpath (1812–79), during the period in which he managed the business, suffered his fair share of setbacks, but he understood the importance of expanding the business which his father had set up. He was involved not just in the wine trade, but also with the importing

The Blandy family graves in the British Cemetery in Funchal

of coal, which his ships brought from England to Madeira. Charles Ridpath's sons, on the other hand, made names for themselves by installing a public mains system for drinking water in Funchal. In addition they published Madeira's first newspaper, the "Diário de Notícias", which still exists today. In 1936 the Blandy family bought the renowned Reid's Hotel, which they kept until the summer of 1996, when it was finally sold to an international hotel chain.

The Blandy's family grave is to be found in the British Cemetery in Funchal.

Winston Churchill
(1874–1965)
British
politician

Among the many famous people who have come to Madeira over the years and learnt to appreciate its mild climate and luxuriant vegetation, Winston Churchill is perhaps pre-eminent. He was born on November 30th 1874 at Blenheim Palace, the son of the Conservative politician, Lord Randolph Churchill. The younger Churchill initially drew attention to himself with his newspaper reports on the Boer War and then in 1900 he embarked on a political career. He went over to the Liberals and from 1906 held various government offices, becoming in 1911 First Lord of the Admiralty, with responsibility for arming the British fleet. After his return to the Conservative camp in 1924, Churchill was first made Chancellor of the Exchequer, in 1939 became First Lord of the Admiralty again, and in 1940, during the Second World War, Prime Minister of an all-party coalition government.

Even today Winston Churchill still symbolises the British spirit of resistance. He became famous, both for his appeals to the British peo-

ple to hold out during German air attacks on British cities, and for his famous "blood, sweat and tears" speech.

In 1949 Winston Churchill visited the island of Madeira for the first time, devoting himself almost exclusively to his hobby of painting. In the fishing village of Câmara dos Lobos, for which he developed a real love, there is a small viewing balcony commemorating the vantage point from where he on more than one occasion painted the colourful hustle and bustle of the harbour. Churchill died on January 24th 1965.

Elisabeth I was born in Munich on December 24th 1837, the second daughter of Duke Maximilian Joseph. As a consequence of a mat-

Elisabeth I
(1837–98)
Empress of
Austria and
Queen of
Hungary

rimonial policy designed to advance German interests she was married to the Austrian Emperor Franz Joseph I and became Empress of Austria and in 1867 Queen of Hungary as well. The issue of this union comprised a son, Rudolph, the heir to the throne, and three daughters, Sophie, Gisela and Marie Valerie. Elisabeth I, who was popularly and affectionately called "Sissi", was gifted, artistic and a sportswoman – but also very stubborn. She showed a strong distaste for the strict etiquette of courtly life, which was to last all her life, and quickly retreated into a spiritual isolation, becoming an outsider in her own court. The rest of her life was characterised by a restless nomadism.

On one of her journeys she came to the island of Madeira, but in a poor state of health (many doctors even thought it was the onset of tuberculosis). For almost half a year she lived at the Quinta das Angústias, located on the site of the present-day Quinta Vigia, the official residence of the president of the regional government. The mild maritime climate of Madeira had an immediate beneficial effect on her health. Driven by her inner unrest she left Madeira again on April 28th 1861 in order to return by an indirect route to the imperial court in Vienna. On September 10th 1898 Elisabeth I was murdered in Geneva by the Italian anarchist Luigi Lucheni. Her life served as a basis for numerous romantic novels,

some of which were turned into films, and of these one was to turn the German actress Romy Schneider into a world star.

Henry (Henrique), born on March 4th 1394 the third son of King João I of Portugal, never actually took part in a long sea voyage but history was later to give him the sobriquet "the Navigator" (o Navegador). The young Infante (heir to the throne) laid his claim to fame by captur-

Henry the
Navigator
(1394–1460)
discoverer

ing Ceuta in 1415. In gratitude the King made him Duke of Viseu and entrusted the defence and government of the captured town to him.

Old sea charts, manuscripts and the tales brought back by returning seafarers awakened an interest in sea travel in the young prince. His appointment as Grand Master of the Order of Knights of Christ gave

him access to the wealth of the disbanded Order of the Knights Templar. This enabled him to turn his seafaring dreams into reality. According to popular tradition he founded a seafaring school at Sagres in the far south-west of Portugal, where new navigating techniques were tried out and passed on to young sailors. At the adjoining wharves a completely new type of ship, the caravel, is thought to have been built. It was far superior to conventional sailing ships in manoeuvrability and seaworthiness.

During the years following, Henry financed many voyages of discovery. First of all the Madeira archipelago was discovered, or rediscovered, and colonised in 1423 (in 1433 Prince Henry received the islands from King Duarte as a feudal payment). The Azores followed and then Henry's ships pushed further and further along the African coast (the "Pepper Coast"), reaching Cape Verde, Gambia and finally Guinea. A crucial part of the driving force behind these voyages of discovery was not just the lure of trade in gold, spices and slaves, but also the battle against Islam. Henry the Navigator must be given the credit for laying the foundation of Portugal's development as a colonial power. He died on November 13th 1460 in Sagres.

Karl I
(1888–1922)
Emperor of
Austria and
King of
Hungary

Karl I, a great-nephew of Emperor Franz Joseph I, was born in Persenbeug in Lower Austria on August 17th 1887. Following the death of his uncle, the heir to the throne, Franz Ferdinand, who was assassinated at Sarajevo on June 28th 1914, Karl ascended the throne as Emperor of Austria and King of Hungary on December 21st 1916. During his unhappy two-year period of rule, which marked the end of the Hapsburg era, the First World War came to an end. In Austrian domestic politics Karl was unsuccessful in tackling decisive reforms. In November 1918, as a result of the pressure imposed by the Russian Revolution of that year, he gave up exercising his governing powers in Austria and Hungary, without formally abdicating. After two failed attempts to re-establish the monarchy in Hungary he was banished to Madeira just before the entente. The last of the Hapsburgs to ascend the imperial throne died on the island on April 1st 1922 of a lung disease. The sarcophagus with his mortal remains now stands in the Church of Nossa Senhora do Monte in Monte.

Christopher
Columbus
(1451–1506)
seafarer and
discoverer

Christopher Columbus is believed to have been born in Genoa in 1451 and became involved in seafaring at a very early age. At the age of 25 he arrived in Lisbon, the Portuguese royal seat and principal port, where he became fascinated by the idea of a western sea route to India, which had been the subject of speculation since ancient times. As his idea of sending an expedition to investigate the possibility of such a route did not receive an encouraging response from the Portuguese royal house, Columbus continued to occupy himself with maritime trade. In 1478 he visited Madeira for the first time in order to buy sugar for a merchant of Genoese origin living in Lisbon. On the island Columbus met Filipa Moniz, the daughter of Bartolomeu Perestrelo, the first Portuguese governor of the neighbouring island of Porto

Santo, whom he married a year or so later. This alliance gave him access to the highest circles of Portuguese society.

Columbus is thought to have lived on Porto Santo from 1479 to 1484 where he probably worked out his plan for a voyage westwards. After the "Junta dos Matemáticos" in Lisbon refused to finance his scheme, Columbus went to Spain. In 1492 he left the harbour at Palos with a small fleet of three ships and three months later he anchored at the Bahaman island of Guanahaní (today San Salvador) and in so doing discovered the American continent, not India as he had hoped. Right up to his death in Valladolid on May 20th 1506 Columbus believed unwaveringly that he had indeed found the westerly sea route to India. Since 1899 the final place of rest of the great sailor has been in Seville, although it is disputed whether his mortal remains really are inside the sarcophagus.

On Porto Santo there is now a house with the name Casa de Colombo which contains a museum. Columbus is said to have lived in this house although there is no historical proof of this.

Even though Madeira is nearly 1000km distant from the Portuguese mainland, the visitor will keep on coming across the Portuguese King Manuel I, who is called the "Great" or the "Fortunate" because of the prosperity and good fortune Portugal enjoyed during his reign. The style of architecture developed during this period and named after Manuel, which incorporated elements of early Renaissance, Moorish Mudéjar style and Oriental-Indian settings, was also employed on the island of Madeira. Manuel I
(1469–1521)
King of
Portugal

Manuel was born in 1469, the youngest son of the Infante Fernando. When the heir to the throne, the Infante Afonso, was killed in a riding accident, Manuel was proclaimed King on October 27th 1495 in Alcácer do Sal.

Manuel used marriage alliances to forge close links with the Spanish royal house. He was first married to Isabella of Castile, the widow of the Infante Afonso. After her death he married her sister María of Castile and by her fathered the heir to the Spanish throne João III. Manuel's third and last wife was Leonor of Castile, who had actually been promised to his own son.

Manuel I took measures to strengthen the power of the throne over the nobility: government administration was centralised and taxes and customs duties standardised. Manuel's reign is linked most of all, however, with the voyages of discovery which the Portuguese monarch promoted, initially out of commercial motives. On his behalf Vasco da Gama discovered the sea route to India and Pedro Alvares Cabral sailed to Brazil. As a consequence Lisbon became the leading merchant port in Europe; untold wealth flowed into the country and this found its visual expression in the architecture of the period.

However Portugal's "Golden Age" was of only short duration: even at the time of Manuel's death – he died in 1521 in Lisbon of a fever – the zenith of Portugal's glory had already been reached.

William Reid, the founder of Reid's Hotel, was born in Scotland in 1822, one of twelve children of an impoverished Scottish peasant. At the age of 14 the sickly boy entered service on a ship travelling from Scotland to Madeira, hoping not just to earn a living but also to improve his health. He first found work with a German baker in Funchal, but then later became involved in the wine trade. At the same time he William Reid
(1822–88)
hotelier

spotted a gap in the market, the realisation of which was to change the rest of his life completely. With his wife Margaret Dewey he rented out furnished gentlemen's houses on Madeira to foreign visitors. Some years later he then built his first hotel, for which he was fortunate enough to have the financial backing of the Duke of Edinburgh. More hotels followed, including the Santa Clara Hotel and Miles Carno Hotel in Funchal.

William Reid did not actually live to see his dream of a luxury hotel for well-to-do visitors come to fruition: he died in 1888 aged 66. His sons Willy and Alfred did have the privilege, however, of opening the hotel that had been their father's brainchild, and Reid's Hotel even today sets a standard of excellence which other hotels on Madeira and further afield seek to match.

Art and Culture

Architecture and Art History

Portugal's economic and cultural flowering, which took place under the rule of King Manuel I (1495–1521) of the Avis dynasty, had its influence on Portuguese architecture. The King gave his name to the Manueline style, which in its formal principles can be compared with the late Gothic style, which originated about the same time. Overall, however, the Manueline style achieved a considerable independence, not least because it contains clearly visible elements of early Renaissance, but also the Moorish Mudéjar style and Oriental-Indian influences.

Examples of the Manueline style can even be found on Madeira.

The fact that Portugal at the time of Henry the Navigator was fast growing into the world's leading maritime power is also reflected in the architecture and artistic creation of the period.

Characteristic of this specifically Portuguese variation in style is a marked delight in décor which – like the Spanish Plateresque style – embodies naturalistic elements borrowed from the world of the sea and seafaring (e.g. knots and coils of rope, mussels, coral, etc.). A particularly beautiful example of this stylistic opulence can be found in the form of a Manueline window in the garden of the Quinta das Cruzes in Funchal.

On Madeira, however, although much was built or decorated in the Manueline style, there is no one building as imposing as, for instance, the Hieronymite Monastery of Belém in Portugal itself. This is probably due not only to the

Manueline stone window in the garden of the Quinta das Cruzes

island's considerable distance from the Portuguese mainland, but even more to its provincial status. Thus a much simpler style of architecture sufficed here which, although it incorporated the basic stylistic elements of the period, remained a long way behind the splendid models of mainland architecture, both in formal richness and decoration.

As the centuries passed, changes in artistic taste came to Madeira as well, although there was often a loyal adherence to old traditional models – perhaps for reasons of cost. A clearly defined change did occur during the Baroque age, however, which during its apex in the 18th c. caused the style to be employed in the renovation of several churches on Madeira. Their interiors, which until then had been maintained in the Manueline or closely related Mudéjar style, were refurbished with all the magnificence of Baroque. There are many examples of the late Baroque style in which altars, walls, niches and ceilings were given wooden embellishments boasting elegant carvings and gold-leaf coatings. Where late Baroque meets the Manueline style the perceptive observer will see a fascinating interaction (e.g. in the Sé, Funchal's cathedral).

A winged altar piece in the Museu de Arte Sacra in Funchal

In painting no significant impulses have come from Madeira

Whereas a relatively independent school of painting developed on mainland Portugal between the 15th and 18th c., the artists who were born or resident on Madeira were not really able to make a contribution to this development. Instead, Madeira's painters derived most of their inspiration from the motherland, noticeably so in the area of sacred painting. No painter from Madeira achieved anything approaching the reputation of such important Portuguese painters as Grão Vasco, Gregório Lopes or Cristóvão de Figueiredo.

The reason there are so many paintings of, for example, Flemish origin in the churches and museums on Madeira is because sugar was such a sought-after trading commodity that some merchants received paintings by famous masters in payment. From about 1472 onwards there was a direct trading link between Madeira and Flanders.

Azulejos: tiny blue treasures

Notwithstanding a certain undeniable similarity between the word "azulejo" and the word for blue in Portuguese "azul", it is in fact the case that the etymological origin of the word "azulejo" has nothing to do with this, but is to be found in the Arabic language, where the word "az-zuleycha" stands for "mosaic stone" or "small polished stone". Azulejos are ceramic tiles which were imported from Spain to Portugal from the beginning of the 16th c. At first the trade was just in relief tiles, which were produced by Moorish workers in blue and other primary colours with geometric patterns. After the Moors were driven out of Spain towards the end of the 16th c. and the supply of their tiles stopped, various people in Portugal got together and started their own azulejo factories (in Lisbon, Oporto and Coimbra and other towns). In these workshops it was not just geometric patterns which were used but also other motives. Not were they any longer made with relief surfaces, but instead were produced as flat tiles following Italian and Flemish models. In addition the baked earthenware tiles were given a white pewter glaze which was painted on with metallic oxide colours.

Azulejos also made their way from the Portuguese mainland to Portuguese colonies and overseas territories. They can be found today in Macao (near Hong Kong) as well as in Madeira and elsewhere.

Azulejo manufacturing enjoyed its heyday during the 17th c. Typical of this time are whole tile-carpets (tapetes) in the colours blue, white and yellow with the most varied pictorial motives. These "carpets" or coverings were used on any surface imaginable – altar panels and side walls in churches, staircases, fountains, benches and the inner and outer walls of gentlemen's houses. They were even used to make decorative street signs.

When the Portuguese royal court had to take refuge in Brazil at the beginning of the 19th c. and the country was torn apart by civil wars, azulejo production came to an almost complete standstill and it was not until the middle of the century that it prospered again. Following a Brazilian fashion, tiles began to be used to decorate whole façades and interior walls of civil, commercial and municipal buildings. A final flowering of the tradition in Portugal occurred at the turn of the century and today in commercial terms it is a relatively unimportant industry.

The large majority of azulejos which can be seen today all over Madeira, date from recent times and are generally mass-produced. Nevertheless they are very pretty to look at – particularly the holy pictures consisting of several small tiles which are found next to entrance doors, or the pictures made with large numbers of tiles which depict rural life on Madeira. There are still some churches with notable azulejo pictures, for instance the Collegium Church in Funchal. The tiles of the spire of the Sé, Funchal's cathedral, date from the 16th c. and are among some of the oldest azulejos on Madeira. Finally there are some sumptuous mosaics made of tiles kept in the Quinta das Cruzes. These were able to be saved when the Convent of Santa Clara, which stood on the site of the present-day Santa Catarina Airport, was pulled down.

The art of forming pictures from small glazed tiles originated in the 16th c.

Language

Portuguese is
a Romance
language

Portuguese belongs to the Romance family of languages but has remained to a large extent isolated. It is spoken on mainland Portugal, the Portuguese Atlantic islands, The Azores and Madeira and in Macao (southern China). The language is also used in the former Portuguese colonies in Africa, India and Indonesia. A slightly modified form of Portuguese is spoken in Brazil by some 115 million people. In all between 125 and 135 million people speak Portuguese and the language is the seventh most spoken language in the world.

The origins of the Portuguese language are to be found in the Lusitanian form of vulgar Latin. Of the other Romance languages, Castilian Spanish is the closest, but the Portuguese language is on the whole much more archaic and conservative. The differences between the various forms of Portuguese in present-day use are moreover far less marked than those of other Western European tongues.

Portuguese lexis is derived mainly from Latin-Romanic. There are only a very few words of Basque or Germanic origin, the latter tending to be of West Gothic provenance. Arabic loan-words are fewer than in Castilian because Portugal was liberated from Moorish rule considerably earlier than Spain.

Written Portuguese and the received pronunciation, which is influenced mainly by the speech of the educated classes in Coimbra and Lisbon, quite early on consciously adopted French, Italian and Spanish elements.

See also Practical Information, Language.

Folklore

Traditional
dress

The traditional costumes once worn by the Madeirans have all but disappeared from everyday life on the island and are now only donned for special occasions. The only people who regularly wear them are the women in the little flower market behind the cathedral in Funchal and the basket-sled drivers at Monte. Their colourful costumes are, however, the result of official prescription – both groups are required to wear these clothes when they are at work. The flower sellers' costume consists of a knee-length striped pleated skirt, a white blouse and an elaborately embroidered waistcoat over which a kind of cape can be worn. The basket-sled drivers' dress is characterised by a straw hat with a black hatband, loosely-cut white trousers and shirts.

Certain features of the Madeirans' original dress can still be seen in everyday life, however. These include the woollen caps (*barrete de lã*) worn by the men, which either have ear-flaps for keeping warm or a tall bobble (in which case it goes under the name of "carapuça"). Other typical features are the goatskin boots with turned-down legs (*botas*), and the white, or occasionally brown, suits, which on special holidays are worn with a red sash around the waist. The women's and girls' costume basically consists of a long red woollen skirt and a white blouse, over which a shawl is thrown – either a single-coloured red one or a brightly-coloured embroidered one.

Music

While the Moorish influence in Spanish folk music is unmistakable, Portugal maintains a certain independence in this respect. This is also true of Madeira, which – apart from short interludes – has been in Portuguese possession for centuries and has always been oriented towards the culture of the motherland. Any influences from other cul-

Flower-sellers behind the Cathedral in Funchal wearing their national costumes

tures, for instance the slaves brought onto the island from the 15th c. onwards, are today only discernible by the expert.

The most characteristic form of popular music on Madeira is the desfaio (also called despique), which is never missing from the many village festivals on the island. It is a kind of antiphonal singing in which two singers in rhyme narrate the events in the life of a village, sometimes even those of a family. Simple instruments, such as the braguinha, a four-stringed instrument rather like a ukelele, are used to accompany these songs, which are designed to arouse plenty of merriment in their listeners. The origin of the desfaio is not entirely clear; a similar form of vocalised narrative is to be found in northern Portugal.

A very special type of Portuguese folk music, which is also cultivated on Madeira, is the fado. Its origins are thought to lie in the folk music of Africa and Brazil, while other musicologists incline to the view that the fado is of Moorish origin. A fado singer (*fadista*) is always accompanied by two guitar players. The songs are of a narrative nature and generally have a profound, sometimes extraordinarily sad intensity. During the rule of the dictator Salazar the fado was officially banned, although it continued to be sung in secret.

Fado

At the many popular religious and secular festivals traditional dances are usually accompanied with song and music, which is played on traditional instruments. On Madeira, as in the rest of Portugal, these include, besides the already mentioned braguinha, guitars (*guitarra, viola*), violin (*rabeca*), flute (*flauta*), drums (*tambor*) or a kind of rattle (*reque-reque*), which probably originated in Africa. A Madeiran speciality, although it actually comes from northern Portugal, is the briquinho, a kind of Turkish crescent: it consists of a wooden bar to

Instruments

Sadness in the Heart, Fire in the Blood

When Ludovina suddenly puts her serving-tray to one side and sits down on a simple wooden stool in the middle of the dining area, most of the visitors at the little restaurant in the old quarter of Funchal know that the high point of the evening awaits them. Everything goes quiet; only the most unavoidable sounds of clinking cutlery and gently clattering crockery still emerge from the kitchen itself. The waitress, who is possibly in her fifties, surveys her dozen or so guests with a long intent gaze and then gives the two men a quick wink. One of them holds a twelve-string melody guitar, the guitarra, while the other places his fingertips on the strings of the viola, the six-string rhythm guitar. As it has now also become quiet in the kitchen and both cooks have come and leant on the doorway, arms folded, Ludovina begins to sing. Softly, with a husky voice, she vividly recounts the story of a love long past. The locals among the guests nod not understandingly and every now and then have a drink of their wine. When the lady in the white overall finishes, an almost deathly hush descends over the room. Then those who have not only heard the words but also internalised them, start to clap with their finger knuckles on the wooden tables, as a sign of their understanding and appreciation of the universalised suffering which Ludovina has expressed in her music.

Many things on Madeira bring to mind the Portuguese mainland, not least the fado, which came from there to the island. In the old quarter of Funchal there are several inns and restaurants where guests sit enthralled by the singing of the fado, generally in a minor key and full of sadness, accompanied just by simple chords on Spanish guitars. The word "fado" is a corruption of the Latin "fatum", which signifies misfortune or fate. The heart of a fado song is the "saudade", which contains feelings which are essentially Portuguese: world-weariness, longing and fatalism. There may be a genuine need to express these feelings, for the once proud nation of seafarers is now one of the poorer countries of Europe. And yet the fado does not always have to be sad, or at least it does not need to end sadly. There are songs in which melancholy has its place, but which then end with an optimistic life-affirming finale.

Only in exceptional circumstances do fado singers perform for a fee. Some of them would regard it as an impertinence to be offered money for something which for them comes spontaneously from the pain and longing of their soul. It can quite often even happen that the first fadista is relieved by a second singer and then this one in turn makes way for yet another. If this is the case then an evening with fado singing can become very long indeed. For each of these singers has something to tell, even if it is only the recent sad experience of the singer's advances being rejected by the girl he aspires to. The fado can be divided into two types, "fado de Lisboa" and "fado de Coimbra". The most plausible explanation of the fado's origins is the one that claims it originated in the nautical world, and certainly rhythmic components of the fado seem to point that way. But possibly the fado is simply what the Portuguese writer Ventura de Abrantes called "the liturgy of the national soul".

which a mechanism is attached which can be moved up and down with the hand. Tiny little dolls in traditional Madeiran dress are attached to this mechanism and during the up and down movement they tap castanet-like wooden beaters and little bells together, thereby providing a rhythm.

The high point of the musical calendar is the Madeira Music Festival (May–June), which attracts famous musical ensembles from all over the world, not least because of the magnificent acoustic of the theatre in Funchal.

Madeira Music Festival

The municipal theatre in Funchal only hosts visiting productions and has no permanent company of its own. From time to time theatre groups come over from Portugal and there are also visits from overseas ensembles.

The minho, which is danced mainly at village celebrations, also comes originally from northern Portugal. It consists of a slow round dance in which the participants lean forward with their heads and the upper parts of their bodies. As they do the steps, they hardly lift their feet up from the ground, causing a shuffling sound. The minho may also possibly have been influenced by the slaves who were brought to Madeira shortly after the arrival of the first Portuguese settlers. The bent posture of the dancers is often thought to be a symbol for the oppression felt by the slaves.

Theatre

The origin of other popular dances can be found in the religious processions which take place throughout the year in a strict Catholic country like Portugal and enjoy a high status. Of special note is the annual folk festival which takes place in Santana in July where the singing and dancing is totally authentic.

Dance

In contrast to the Portuguese mainland, where men of letters such as Luís Vaz de Camões (1524–80) have attained a pre-eminent place in world literature, the art of writing has always had rather a sketchy existence on Madeira. The only writer to have achieved distinction is the Madeira-born poet Francisco Álvares de Nóbrega (1773–1807), who won himself the nickname of 'little Camões'.

Literature

Arts and Crafts

The origins of the embroidery tradition on Madeira date back to the 16th c. when the high levels of skills of Madeiran women were already famous. Tablecloths with innumerable variations, beautifully decorated serviettes and handkerchiefs, or even whole tapestries, all have found their way from Madeira to the rest of the world. Even in the most aristocratic homes the quality of the islanders' handiwork has been much prized. However it is often forgotten that embroidery for many families on Madeira represents an indispensable contribution to their household income and at least 20,000 women on the island live off the proceeds of their needlework.

Madeiran embroidery

Even today over half of all the embroidery is produced in the home; the textiles used, however, are first prepared in the factory and then sent back there for the "finishing touches". Unlike in earlier times, the patterns are no longer applied by hand but are perforated into the cloth using a machine, the "máquina de picotar". The patterns are in many cases a strongly guarded secret of the "bordadeiras", the embroideresses, and are passed on from generation to generation.

Whereas up until the middle of the 19th c. embroidery was done exclusively for domestic use, in about 1850 the foundation was laid

Most needlework is done at home – the traditional patterns being handed down from one generation to another

for the first industrial production of embroidery. Elizabeth (Bella) Phelps, the daughter of an English missionary, is responsible for the first examples of the Madeiran women's handicraft reaching England. They attracted enormous attention at the Great Exhibition in London in 1851.

The traditional embroidery of Madeira had its heyday at the beginning of this century. In the 1930s industrial embroidery was introduced and this meant that the patterns were copied in large quantities and then delivered to the embroiderers. After the Second World War there was a marked downturn in exports; the islanders' reply to this challenge was to raise the quality standards for embroidery. In 1978 the Instituto de Bordados, Tapeçaria e Artesanato da Madeira (I.B.T.A.M.) was founded, an institute for arts and crafts on Madeira. Its aims are to provide a training leading to qualifications and payment for the embroiderers according to the quality of their work; it awards a seal of quality and organises embroidery sales throughout the world.

The basket-makers of Camacha

The basket-makers of Madeira also enjoy an excellent reputation, particularly those from the tiny village of Camacha in the east of the island. Although the raw material grows at many places on Madeira, especially in the damp valleys along the north coast, Camacha is the centre of the basket-making industry. Like the embroidery tradition, basket-making on Madeira dates back to the middle of the 16th c. when baskets were needed to transport goods and loads, although the industrialised production that we know today was not introduced until the 19th c. The basketwork is woven from special kinds of willow cane, a cross between *Salix alba* and *Salix fragiles*. After the harvest the canes are stripped in a very labour-intensive process and then boiled in large tubs, at which stage they acquire their typical brown colouring. The introduction of machines into the weaving process is not possible, so each piece produced is unique.

A tour round the Café Relógio in Camacha, which is where the basketwork produced in the village is sold, reveals the variety of goods available. The range extends from tiny bread baskets to washing and shopping baskets and even complete suites of furniture. Small pieces of artistic basket-weaving are increasingly popular, e.g. copies of animals. The threat of increasing competition is causing the basket-weaving families of Camacha concern. Although the I.B.T.A.M., the institute for arts and crafts, promotes training opportunities for the basket-makers, there is – in contrast to the embroiderers – no quality seal. The number of people engaged in the work has also seen a noticeable decrease; young people in particular are seeking a less arduous and more remunerative form of employment.

A selection of cane furniture for sale in the Café Relógio in Camacha

Madeira in Quotations

Joseph Banks
(1744–1820)
British naturalist

The climate is so fine that any man might wish it was in his power to live there under the benefits of English laws and liberty.

Journal of the Rt. Hon. Sir Joseph Banks, 1768

Richard Burton
(1821–90)
British Explorer

Madeira . . . has, and ever will have, one terrible drawback besides extensive humidity. The ennui which it breeds is peculiar; it makes itself felt during a few hours' stay. Little islands are all large prisons: one cannot look at the sea without wishing for the wings of the swallow. This, with usual sense of confinement, combines the feeling of an hospital, or a sick-bay, and one soon sighs to escape from its dreary volcanic rocks. . . . In the season there are balls, concerts, teafights; out of season, nothing. The theatre is built, but rarely speaks; the opera has to take root; the Turkish bath is unknown; indeed, there is not a bath on the island. Even the English club-rooms are closed at night. I should feel in such a place like a caged hawk; or, to speak more classically, like a Prometheus with the Demon Despair gnawing at my heart.

Wanderings in West Africa, 1863

Baedeker's
Madeira
(1934)

Madeira can be visited all the year round on account of its mild temperate climate. Those suffering from illnesses or in need of recuperation will be able to enjoy a cool and pleasant stay here in the height of summer (those with severe lung diseases are excluded).

Anyone travelling abroad should always be aware that he is a representative of his country and that his appearance and behaviour will have an influence on the opinion that people will have of his countrymen. Good form and etiquette are the best advertisement, both for the individual and for his country. He should pay attention to his bearing and dress, as these are the things by which he is judged. It should always be borne in mind that in Spain and Portugal, with their well-developed sense of equality, even the most humble man will expect to be treated like a "caballero". Overfamiliarity, on the other hand, is always out of place. The sensitive national pride of both the Spanish and the Portuguese is very easy to wound; therefore one should hold back in any political discussions and refrain from criticising their national characteristics.

From Madeira, Canary Islands, Azores, west coast of Morocco. Guidebook by Karl Baedeker; Leipzig (1934).

Winston
Churchill
(1874–1965)
British
politician

Ladies and gentlemen, here is a famous wine indeed, vintaged when Marie Antoinette was still alive.

Remark by the British politician during his stay on Madeira in January 1950, when he opened a bottle of Madeira wine of the 1792 vintage.

Bernard Shaw with his wife and dance instructor Max Rinder

To the only man who ever taught me anything.

George Bernard
Shaw
(1856–1950)
Irish writer

*Dedication on a photograph which the Irish writer presented to Max
Rinder, the dance instructor at Reid's Hotel. Rinder taught the 68-year-
old Shaw the steps to the tango while the latter was staying at Reid's
Hotel from December 30th 1924 to February 12th 1925.*

Suggested Routes

The following recommendations should serve as general guidelines for people visiting Madeira for the first time and will enable them to make their stay on the island as memorable as possible and to be sure of not missing the many scenic delights of the island. The names of sights and places printed in bold refer to specific entries in the "Sights from A to Z" section, which is to be found in the main body of the book. In all cases the distances given in kilometres refer to the most straightforward route.

The roads on Madeira are in good condition, though often narrow and steep with many bends. Side roads sometimes only have a cobbled surface. As a general rule, therefore, the motorist should not exceed 80km. per hour.

Condition of roads

Funchal–Monte–Faial–Funchal (Half-day trip; about 35km)

The good quality road no. 103 leads northwards from Funchal and continues along many twists and turns upwards between gardens and villas full of flowers to the village of ★★**Monte** 8km to the north in the middle of magnificent plane and oak woods. The most famous sight at Monte is the Church of Nossa Senhora do Monte which contains the sarcophagus of the Hapsburg Emperor Karl I and a remarkable statue of the Madonna which on Ascension Day is the focal point of a large procession. Among the sights of Monte the superb tropical gardens (7 hectares in area) must take pride of place. From Monte the 103 continues on to ★★**Ribeiro Frio**, a tiny village consisting of just a few houses, but which has become well known because of its trout farm. A good half-hour's drive further on along the 103 is the unassuming little village of **Faial** on the north coast of the island. It lies 150m above sea level, has about 1500 inhabitants and is surrounded by vine terraces and fields of sugar cane and vegetables. There is a good view from the church terrace, as well as from a special viewpoint just outside Faial, from which it is possible to see the ★★**Ponta de São Lourenço** peninsula and the neighbouring island of ★★**Porto Santo**. The return journey to Funchal follows the outward route.

Funchal–Monte

Monte–Ribeiro Frio

Ribeiro Frio–Faial

Funchal–Curral das Freiras–Funchal (Half-day trip; 14km)

The road no. 105 leaves Funchal in a north-westerly direction and after 3km reaches the village of ★**São Martinho** with its noteworthy church (inside it contains an 18th c. silver processional cross and various elaborately embroidered robes).
The route continues along the 105 in the direction of Santo António, but at the village of Chamarra it leaves the 105, taking the 107 to reach the viewpoint of **Eira do Serrado** (Serrado saddle; alt. 1025m) on the north-east edge of ★★**Pico Serrado**. Here a road (1km) turns off right to the Miradouro. The car park is surrounded by stalls selling souvenirs of all kinds. A pleasant shaded forest path leads in about 10 minutes to the viewing platform high over the Curral valley. The view from vertiginous heights down into the deep valley bottom, sur-

Funchal–São Martinho

◀ Deep channels made by millions of years erosion

53

São Martinho –Pico dos Barcelos

rounded by steep walls of rock, is one of the most marvellous experiences Madeira has to offer. Continue another 3km upwards through mountain scenery full of trees and flowers to reach the Miradouro Pico dos Barcelos (alt. 355m). The viewing terrace, which is surrounded by a magnificent array of flowers, offers a superb view of the south coast of Madeira if the weather is reasonably clear.

Recommended detour to Pico Serrado

From the nearby peak of Pico Serrado (literally "sawn-off summit"; alt. 1115m) the visitor will get what is probably the most magnificent view across the whole of Madeira's central mountain chain from **Pico Ruivo de Santana** (1861m) and **Pico de Arieiro** (1818m) in the east to Pico Grande (1607m) and Pico do Jorge (1692m) in the west.

Eiro do Serrado –Curral das Freiras

On the other side of the saddle the road winds down a number of hairpin bends and through some tunnels until after 4km it reaches the fertile valley floor, surrounded by high walls of rock, of the ★★ **Curral das Freiras** (stable of the nuns) or Gran Curral. The village of Curral das Freiras (alt. 690m) is situated on the rock-strewn bed of the Ribeira dos Socorridos, like an oasis in the middle of a desert of stone.

Alternative:
Walk from Eiro do Serrado to Curral das Freiras

The old winding mule track, cobbled for the most part, leads from the car park at Eira do Serrado down to the village of Curral das Freiras. Until 1959 it was the only route connecting the Curral valley with Funchal. The walk, which takes about an hour in each direction, is very enjoyable.

Funchal–Câmara de Lobos–São Vicente–Funchal (Day trip)

Funchal–Pico da Ponta da Cruz

Leave Funchal in a westerly direction either on the motorway or on the scenic coast road, which immediately starts to skirt around the southern slopes of Pico da Ponta da Cruz (alt. 263m; good viewpoint), an old crater not far from the mountain of the same name. After another 3 km ★ **Câmara de Lobos** (wolf's gorge) is reached, a small picturesquely situated fishing village at the eastern foot of Cabo Girão, much visited by artists (including Winston Churchill). Beyond Câmara de Lobos the road starts to climb upwards and gradually winds its way away from the coast in order to skirt round the northern side of Cabo Girão. The next stop is **Estreito da Câmara de Lobos**, a village famous for its wine. Every year in the autumn there is a wine festival at harvest time lasting several days. The Sunday market with its colourful hustle and bustle is well worth visiting. From Estreito da Câmara de Lobos a side road 4km northwards leads to the Quinta Jardim da Serra with a fine view.

Estreito da Câmara de Lobos

Estreito da Câmara de Lobos –Cabo Girão–

About 4km further on from Estreito da Câmara de Lobos a road turns off left to the viewpoint for ★★ **Cabo Girão** (see Estreito da Câmara de Lobos). The cliff which plunges 589m down to the sea is said to be the highest in Europe. From the viewpoint there is an awe-inspiring panorama encompassing a series of well-established terraced fields which seem to grow ever smaller as they descend.

Cabo Girão– Campanário

The coast road very quickly reaches the village of Campanário, pleasantly situated on the side of the mountain. The 17th c. church is the only point of interest. From here it is roughly another 6km to ★ **Ribeira Brava**, a little fishing town in a pretty location at the mouth of the mountain stream of the same name. It is worth visiting the charming church of São Bento, one of the oldest on the island, whose blue and white steeple roof can be seen from some distance.

Campanário– Ribeira Brava

Ribeira Brava– São Vicente

The road no. 104 to ★ **São Vicente** leaves Ribeira Brava in a northerly direction, climbing inland, mostly along the west bank of the Ribeira Brava and eventually reaches some impressive mountain scenery. After about 12km it passes the Pousada dos Vinháticos (660m), much frequented by local people, situated in a wooded location with a good view. It is a starting-point for a number of superb mountain walks (e.g. to Pico Grande, Pico do Jorge, Pico Ruivo).

Pousada dos Vinháticos

Route 1
Route 2
Route 3
Route 4
Route 5

★ **São Vicente**, the destination on this trip, was originally a simple fishing village but in the past few years it has been discovered by tourists. The Capela de São Roque, built in 1692, with its Baroque façade decorated by pebbled mosaics, is worth seeing. The return journey to Funchal follows the route described above.

Funchal–Paúl da Serra–São Vicente–Santana–Funchal (92km)

For this all-day trip leave Funchal in a westerly direction along the coast road no. 101 and go through ★ **Câmara de Lobos**, ★ **Ribeira Brava** to ★ **Ponta do Sol**, the first stopping-place. Ponta do Sol has 6000 inhabitants; the picturesque village lies on either side of the stream bearing the same name. Like many churches on Madeira the Church of Nossa Senhora da Luz dates back to the 15th c., but later underwent radical alterations, mainly in the 18th c. Just 2km up above Ponta do Sol at Lombada, in the middle of extensive banana plantations, is the Quinta of João Esmeraldo, a travelling companion of Christopher Columbus, who is thought to have established large sugar cane plantations here in the 15th c. The estate residence is now used as a school. Not far to the west of Ponta do Sol is the little fishing village of **Madalena do Mar**. It was founded in 1457 by a certain Henrique Alemão (Henry the German). It is thought that this name may have been a pseudonym used by King Ladislaus III of Poland who is supposed to have lived in exile on Madeira. About 5km beyond Ponta do Sol a side road turns off to the north and leads, after turning westwards a little further on, onto the high plateau of ★ **Paúl da Serra** and then back to the coast road, which it rejoins a little south of Santa. The misty plateau of Paúl da Serra (= mountain swamp; alt. 1300–1400m) extends over an area of 102sq.km and offers quite an unusual contrast to the scenic variety to be found elsewhere on Madeira. The road across the plateau with its various viewpoints offers walkers excellent starting-points for beautiful walks and hikes through the mountains. At the western end there is a road off to the right leading to **Rabaçal**, a small collection of holiday homes.

From Rabaçal there are excellent walks to the Risco waterfalls (1 hr there and back) or to the Vinte-e-cinco Fontes (25 springs; 2 hrs there and back). A short distance to the north-east is the "Balcão" (balcony) with a superb view over the Risco waterfall and close by across the green gorge of the Vinte e Cinco Fontes (gorge of the 25 springs).

(margin notes:)
Funchal–Ponta do Sol

Madalena do Mar

Paúl da Serra

Rabaçal

*Walk to the Risco waterfalls

Suggested Routes

Nossa Senhora de Loreto	Following the coast road no. 101 for another 5km, the Mozarabic-Manueline chapel of Nossa Senhora de Loreto dating from the 16th c. comes into view; it is the scene of a pilgrimage every year on September 8th. Below the coast road, in amongst banana plantations and
Calheta	vine terraces is the little harbour of ★**Calheta**, once the centre of sugar cane growing on Madeira; there is an elaborately carved wooden roof in the choir of the church (1639). From Calheta a side road goes past the Arco da Calheta (846m) viewpoint and on to the Rabaçal refuge
Estreito da Calheta	hut. The coast road now takes a circuitous route upwards to **Estreito da Calheta** with its 16th c. Manueline Capela dos Reis Magos (Chapel of the Three Kings; beautiful paintings on wood). A side road leads from Estreito da Calheta steeply upwards to the charmingly situated Jardim do Mar.
Prazeres	The main route continues on to Prazeres, situated on a wooded plateau with magnificent views. Around the village can be seen the original natural stone houses of basalt which were typical of this part of
Fajão/ Paúl do Mar	Madeira. After 6km a side road turns off left to the village of Fajão da Ovelha, situated at the foot of a massive rock face, surrounded by woods, and to the fishing village of Paúl do Mar, which also cowers beneath a high rock face.
Ponta do Pargo	After another 9km the 101 reaches ★**Ponta do Pargo** (alt. 473m), the most westerly village on the island, which serves an area of Madeira which is one of the richest in traditions. The beautiful old traditional costumes are still worn here on public holidays. From here a single-track road leads to the lighthouse with a good view across the western tip of the island. There is also a footpath from the village which leads down to the Praia do Pesqueiro, the fisherman's beach, surrounded by cliffs. Passing through Achadas da Cruz the road reaches after 14km Santa Maria Madalena, a long extended village, which today is just called Santa for short. Eventually, after numerous hairpin
Porto do Moniz	bends, the road descends to the sea and after 7km reaches ★★**Porto do Moniz**, the village which is at the furthest point on the island from Funchal. If the weather is favourable the rock pools here are excellent for bathing. The tiny pockets of land used for growing vines are a feature of the landscape around Porto Moniz. The route now proceeds eastwards along the northern coast of the island, keeping to the sea. The road, which is often cut deep into the cliffs, is impressive in engineering terms and also exciting, often reducing to just one track through tunnels, as well as passing underneath waterfalls.
São Vicente to Santana	The next destination in this circular trip along the scenically spectacular northern coast is ★**São Vicente** with its carefully restored old quarter. From here the road continues to ★★**Santana**. Its houses, with their roofs coming down to the ground, are typical of the Comarca de Santana and of interest to the visitor. **Faial**, situated just a few kilometres away, possesses a picturesque old quarter and every year is the destination for an important "romaria" (pilgrimage). The 103 then passes through ★**Ribeiro Frio** and ★★**Monte** on its way back to Funchal.

Funchal–São Vicente–Machico–Funchal (Day trip: 90km)

Ponta Delgada	Leave Funchal in a westerly direction on the coast road no. 101 and travel through ★**Câmara de Lobos** to ★**Ribeira Brava**. From here the 104 goes in a northerly direction through often superb scenery to ★**São Vicente**. Here there is a choice between taking the 101 to the left and proceeding on to ★★**Porto do Moniz**, or going in the opposite direction to ★**Ponta Delgada**. Ponta Delgada is a village delightfully

Picturesque view of the coloured fishing boats in Camara de Lobos ▶

Bananas are one of the most important natural products of Madeira

situated on a promontory between orange groves and sugar cane plantations. Besides having a simple white church and a sea-water swimming bath, the village is famous for its "romaria", which takes place every year on the first Saturday in September.

Once past the village, the road leaves the sea behind and describes a broad arc inland. After 2km it passes through the village of

Boaventura

Boaventura. The countryside here is notable for its fruit and willow plantations, the latter being used in the local basket-making industry. The village is a good starting-point for some beautiful walks, especially the one to ★★ **Curral das Freiras**.

Arco de São Jorge

Continuing along the 101 there is a viewpoint, just beyond Arco de São Jorge, which offers a rightly famed view of the north coast.

São Jorge

The village of ★ **São Jorge** has a 17th c. Baroque church with notable altar pictures. From nearby Ponta de São Jorge there is yet another view across the north coast as far as Porto Moniz in the west and Porto da Cruz in the east.

Santana

★★ **Santana**, the main town in the comarca of Santana, is reached after a few kilometres; this is the most fertile area of the island. With its thatched houses surrounded by stunning flowers it must be one of the most picturesque places in the whole of Madeira.

Recommended detour

From Santana it is possible to make an attractive detour to the refuge Casa das Queimadas (alt. 883m) and then on foot southwards to the Parque das Queimadas on the slopes of **Pico Ruivo** (1861m), which can be climbed from here and, when the visibility is really good, offers a fabulous panorama across the mountains of Madeira.

Penha de Aguia

Beyond Santana the coast road continues close to the sea and offers many beautiful views. A striking feature of the landscape is encountered just beyond **Faial** – the strangely shaped 594m high rock Penha de Aguia (eagle's rock).

The little fishing village of ★**Porto da Cruz** lies at the foot of massive cliffs and possesses a small beach of ashes. The village is also well-known for having one of the last distilleries on Madeira in which "aguardente" is produced from sugar cane.

Porto da Cruz

Beyond Porto da Cruz the road turns inland from the sea and goes southwards up into the mountains, reaching the Portela pass at an altitude of 662m. The view from here extends to Porto da Cruz and the bay at Machico.

Portela Pass

From the Portela pass the road EN 102 leads through magnificent wooded mountain scenery to the basket-making village of ★**Camacha** and then directly back to Funchal (30km).

Short cut to Funchal

If the longer route is taken, the road no. 101 is followed first to Santo António da Serra, a well-known health resort, and then on to ★Machico. This little town was once the seat of government of the eastern part of the island of Madeira. From that time date parts of the Cristo chapel, which over the years has had to be rebuilt on numerous occasions owing to flood damage.

Machico

From Machico the road continues on to ★**Santa Cruz** with its note-worthy church dating from the 16th c. After passing Santa Catarina Airport it reaches ★**Caniço**, where it is worth making a short detour to see the monumental statue of Christ. In the village itself the main place of interest is the imposing Baroque church dating from the 18th c.

Santa Cruz

From Caniço it is just a few kilometres to Funchal, the starting-point of this memorable circular trip.

**Sights
from A to Z**

Água de Penha   C 7

Location: 21km north-east of Funchal
Altitude: 2–30m
Population: about 6000

Location and importance

The little village of Água de Penha was specifically targeted for development in the 1970s when tourism underwent large-scale expansion on Madeira. It is situated just a few kilometres from Santa Cruz and is therefore close to Santa Catarina Airport. Inevitably this location has brought with it what could be perceived as the drawback of a large and ambitious luxury tourist development which is hardly one of the quietest on the island. It is intended that after the extension of the runways has been completed at the airport – work on which is currently in progress – Água de Penha should cease to develop any further as a tourist resort and instead should become a "satellite town" of Machico.

Sights

Miradouro Francisco Álvares de Nóbrega

In Água de Penha a road turns off right to the Miradouro Francisco Álvares de Nóbrega (about 1km). The viewpoint offers a fine panorama of the bay of Machico (see entry) and of Ponta de São Lourenço (see entry). Francisco Álvares de Nóbrega (1773–1807), after whom the viewpoint is named, was one of the most famous poets to have been born on Madeira and even today is fondly referred to as "little Camões" – an allusion to the great Portuguese poet. De Nóbrega used his poetic gifts to write satirical verses criticising the Catholic church. This earned him imprisonment at Lepra where he fell ill and his persecution by the inquisition only ended when the poet committed suicide at the age of 34.

Boaventura   B 6

Location: 51km north of Funchal
Altitude: 5–150m
Population: 3000

Location and importance

Beyond the village of São Jorge (see entry) the road leaves the sea in order to describe a wide arc inland. 2km further on it passes the village of Boaventura, which nestles between fields of fruit and extended willow plantations which serve the local basket-making industry. This area is particularly fertile because of its excellent water supply, as several small rivers originating in the central mountains empty into the sea here. During the willow harvest it is possible to see the canes, after they have been cut, being boiled in enormous tubs, which gives them their typical brown colouring.

A good starting-point for walks

While there are no sights of interest in Boaventura itself, the village makes a good starting-point for some beautiful walks. One such leads along an old footpath into the river valley of the Ribeira do Porco and up to the Pico das Torrinhas (alt. 1509m). A more extended walk can be made from Boaventura to Curral das Freiras (see entry).

◀ *The Pico de Arieiro: when it is misty in the valleys, the tops of the mountains are in sunshine*

Boca da Encumeada (Mountain pass)   B/C 4

Location: 21km north-east of Funchal
Altitude: 1004m

The pass of Boca da Encumeada is situated at a height of 1004m on   Location
the no. 104, a good quality road which goes from Ribeira Brava northwards to São Vicente.

Provided the visibility is reasonably clear and the clouds do not lie too   ★★View
low, the viewpoint affords magnificent vistas of the Serra de Água
(1405m) and the Pico Grande (1657m).
    From the top of the pass a footpath leads westwards to the area of
the Paúl da Serra (see entry) and the refuge hut of Rabaçal.

Cabo Girão

See Estreito de Câmara de Lobos

Calheta   C 2

Location: 62km north-west of Funchal
Altitude: 2–230m
Population: about 5500

Calheta is situated in the south-western part of Madeira and can be   Location and
reached from Funchal by the good-quality road no. 101. Calheta used   importance
to be the centre of sugar cane growing on Madeira, but the only remaining evidence of this part of the town's history is provided by the
Moinho de Açúcar, a ruined sugar mill not far from the beach, and a
distillery, which is still used to produce the local sugar-based spirit
known as "aguardente". The town is also well-known for its extensive
vine-growing areas and its cereal farming.

Calheta is demonstrably one of the oldest settlements on Madeira   History
and as early as 1502 it received its town charter. João Gonçalves
Zarco, the rediscoverer of Madeira, is supposed to have assigned
large tracts of agricultural land here to his children, who in turn realised that it was possible to use volcanic ash to increase the land's
fertility. In later times Calheta had its own customs post where the
receipts for Madeira's sugar exports were collected. With the decline
of the Madeiran sugar industry in the 19th c. Calheta lost much of its
former importance.

Sights

The parish church, parts of which date back to 1430, was substantially   ★★Parish church
rebuilt in 1639. The choir contains an interesting wooden roof, elaborately constructed in the Mudéjar style. It is considered one of the
finest examples still extant on Madeira of this type of oriental style of
ornamentation developed by the Christian Moors in Spain. Also of
note is an ebony tabernacle with silver inlays donated by King
Manuel I.

Places of
interest nearby

From Calheta a single-track road leads past the viewpoint Arco da Calheta (alt. 846m) and on to the refuge hut of Rabaçal.

It is also worth taking a detour to Estreito da Calheta (see entry) with its Capela dos Reis Magos (Three kings' chapel).

Camacha   C 6

Location: 15km north-east of Funchal
Altitude: about 715m
Population: about 6300

Location and
importance

Camacha is situated in the eastern part of Madeira and is chiefly known for its basket-making. Almost every one of its 6300 inhabitants is involved in this trade in some way or other. Basket-making can be traced back to the initiative of English merchants who settled on the island in the 19th c. Everywhere in Camacha the long bundles of willow canes can be seen outside the houses for basket-making is very much a home-based industry. It enjoyed a boom on Madeira just after the Second World War when the demand for wickerwork furniture and other articles increased all over Europe.

After a sharp decline in the 1970s, when production costs rose dramatically, while profits slumped, there has been a recent renaissance in the basket-making tradition. This can certainly be attributed to the increase in tourists, as well as to the introduction of modern technology and machines for harvesting and processing the willow canes. In addition, under the guidance of the state arts and crafts institute I.B.T.A.M., there has been a revival of traditional weaving techniques.

Weaving baskets is laborious work – young people in Camacha seek an easier job

Sights

The simply built houses of Camacha, which cluster round the attrac-
tively laid out Largo da Achada, the central village square, are quite
unassuming. In many of the houses the basket weavers can be seen
at their work and they are only too happy for visitors to watch.

   On the square, which is lined with restaurants serving regional specialities and souvenir shops, there is a plaque commemorating a football match which took place in 1875 in Madeira and was thus the first
ever to be played in Portugal. A gentleman called Harry Hinton is
credited with having brought a football over to the island, thereby
initiating the great tradition of Portuguese football.

   ★ Townscape

On the edge of the village square stands the Café o Relógio, which in
earlier times was the fashionable residence of a British merchant family. The clocktower looks unusual – possibly built to look like Big Ben
in London – and is fondly thought of as a symbol for Camacha. Today
the café houses the salerooms of the Madeira basketwork exporters,
who send the basket-makers' products all over the world. On the bottom floor there is a exhibition workshop, where during normal opening hours demonstrations are given of how baskets, chairs and even
complete suites of furniture are woven.

Café o Relógio

From the far end of the village square, the Largo da Achada, there is a
wonderful view over the south-east coast of Madeira.

★ Viewpoint

Câmara de Lobos

D 5

Location: 15km east of Funchal
Altitude: 0–205m
Population: about 5000

Câmara de Lobos (wolf's gorge) is a small fishing village at the eastern foot of Cabo Girão, which for many years has been much frequented by artists. Winston Churchill was once a visitor here and he
found the scenery so delightful that he captured it in several paintings. The village owes its name to the monk seals (Portuguese "lobo"
= wolf) which once used to inhabit the bay. The village is one of the
oldest settlements on Madeira, having been founded by João
Gonçalves Zarco in 1420.

Location and importance

   Câmara de Lobos is the main centre on the island for fishing, in
particular the espada, which is fished here at night from depths of
over 800m and then auctioned at the harbour in the early hours of the
morning. The vines which are cultivated in and around Câmara de
Lobos have one of the best locations in the whole island. While the
men are either engaged in sea fishing or in vine-growing, the women
work at home on embroidery.

   Unfortunately what was once such a romantic place has lost some
of its atmosphere and the sometimes impoverished circumstances in
which the fishermen of Câmara de Lobos and their families have to
live means that the visitor is liable to encounter children begging.

Sights

The old quarter with its maze of alleyways and tiny squares is perched
on the crest of rock known as the Ilhéu, which overlooks the harbour
bay. Many of the old fishermen's houses which cling to the steep rock

★★ Townscape

Câmara de Lobos

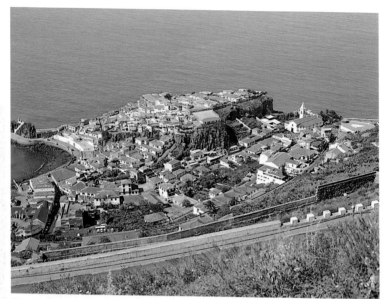

The picturesque fishing town of Câmara de Lobos seen from the road high above

slopes have been renovated in recent years or are at present in the process of being renovated. The best view of the little harbour is from the spot where Churchill sat and painted; it is marked with a plaque.

Igreja São Sebastião (parish church)

At the western end of the old quarter stands the parish church, the Igreja São Sebastião, part of which dates back to around 1430. In the 18th c. the church was restored and decorated with beautiful gilded wooden carvings as well as azulejos.

★Harbour

From the nearby square by the shore there is a narrow promenade which leads eastwards by the sea to the small idyllic harbour. Here there are a large number of colourful fishing boats which are still built in the old traditional way on a small wharf in the harbour.

★Capela Nossa Senhora dos Pescadores

At the harbour stands the chapel of Nossa Senhora dos Pescadores, which from the outside is rather unprepossessing. It was built in 1702 on the site of the first chapel on the island to be erected by Zarco. It is lavishly decorated with gold-painted carvings and paintings.

★Pico da Torre

The hilltop just north-east of the town known as Pico da Torre (205m) offers an excellent view of the town and harbour bay.

Places of interest nearby

Beyond Câmara de Lobos the road starts to climb upwards and, twisting and turning, gradually leaves the coast behind. It then skirts northwards round the rocky cliff of Cabo Girão (see Estreito de Câmara de Lobos).

Above Câmara de Lobos and only a few kilometres distant lies the village of Estreito de Câmara de Lobos (see entry).

Caniçal

Location: 32km east of Funchal
Altitude: 0–50m
Population: about 2000

Today Caniçal is a small and almost insignificant village in the east of Madeira but in previous times it was closely connected with the whaling trade which used to go on in the waters around Madeira. Since 1981 the fishing has been discontinued but up until then as many as 300 whales were caught and slaughtered each year. Since then an area of sea measuring 200,000sq.km has been turned into a national maritime conservation area.

Location and importance

Until the completion of a tunnel in 1956, the former whaling station could only be reached by ship or over the mountains on foot. Similarly, before this time, all that the farmers could do in this dry, desert-like area, whose climatic conditions resemble those of the nearby island of Porto Santo rather than the rest of Madeira, was to rear a few sheep and goats on meagre pastureland. In order to further the economic development of this arid region the government established a free trade zone here with a port. Today the fishermen at Caniçal mostly earn their living by tuna fishing, while some make souvenirs, although no longer from whalebone.

Sights

After Portugal acceded to the international ban on whaling in 1981, leading to the cessation of the trade on Madeira, a small whaling museum was set up in 1990 which uses documents, photographs and

★★Museu da Balaia (Whaling museum)

From the great days of whaling off Madeira – a model of a sperm whale in the small museum

whalebone carvings to provide a reminder of the former trade. Particularly impressive is the reproduction of a sperm whale, while the whalers' boat, named Canoa, which has been placed alongside it,

makes clear the disparity in size between the animal and its hunters. There is a video film which describes the efforts of the Madeiran government in the fields of nature and environmental protection. On a wall in the entrance area hang pictures painted by children, protesting against whale fishing (open: Tue.–Fri. 10am–noon, 1–5pm; Sat., Sun. and holidays until 6pm; entrance charge).

Children's paintings protesting against whaling

Capela da Senhora da Piedade

Beyond Caniçal can be seen the Capela da Senhora da Piedade, situated on an old volcanic cone. It is the destination of a large water procession held every year during the third weekend in September. A small image of the Madonna, which is kept in the chapel and is thought to be the work of a 16th c. Flemish master, is carried to Caniçal and then accompanied on water back to the chapel by a festive procession of boats.

Prainha Beach

At the foot of the hill where the chapel stands, and easily reached in a few minutes on foot, there is a small beach called Prainha which is very popular with local people. It is the only sandy beach on the whole island and therefore tends to be much frequented at weekends.

Caniço (Sítio da Vargem)　　　　　　　　　　　　D 6

Location: 10km east of Funchal
Altitude: 25–200m
Population: about 8000

Location and importance

The little town of Caniço (also known as Sítio da Vargem) is situated only a few kilometres east of Funchal on road no. 101 on either side of the Caniço River. The population of about 8000 today lives mainly from fruit and vegetable growing, hence the large numbers of greenhouses to be seen all around the town.

The narrow river had a special importance in past times: it separated the two administrative areas of Madeira which were set up by the first Portuguese immigrants after the island's discovery by João Gonçalves Zarco. This meant that until the "reunification" in the 18th c. Caniço had two churches and two separate parishes. On the left bank of the river the Church of the Holy Spirit was built, while on the right bank a church was consecrated to St Anthony.

Sights

★Church of the Holy Spirit and St Anthony

On the bustling village square, with its basalt mosaic paving, stands the parish church dating from the 18th c. Over the portal can be seen a sign showing that it is consecrated to the Holy Spirit and St Anthony. This is a reminder of the old feudal border between Machico and Funchal when Caniço was divided into two parishes. When the two communities were brought together in the 18th c., the old dilapidated churches were knocked down and the present one constructed in the Baroque style.

The Manueline chapel of Madre de Deus, dating from the 16th c., also stands on the village square.

Capela Madre de Deus

On the southern edge of the village can be found the Quinta Splendida, a former country house which has been lovingly converted into a hotel and fitted out with antiques to appeal to the visitor with discerning tastes. The beautifully laid out park is also worth seeing.

★Quinta Splendida

Extending along the coast about 3km below Caniço is the new hotel complex of Caniço de Baixo. It is possible to bathe in the sea here, as swimming pools, in which it is possible to go diving as well, have been built into the rock. They are not just open to hotel guests but also to the general public.
Bathing is also possible at the eastern end of the complex and at the little pebble beach of Reis Magos.

Caniço de Baixo

From Caniço a steep road winds down to Ponta do Garajau, where there is a large statue of Christ which was erected in 1927. There is a fine view from the terrace.

★Ponta do Garajau

The section of sea by Ponta do Garajau has been declared a conservation area and called the "Reserva Natural Parcial do Garajau". It extends from Ponta da Oliveira in the east to São Gonçalo in the west.

National maritime park

Curral das Freiras   C 5

Location: 20km north of Funchal
Altitude: 690–990m
Population (in the village of Curral das Freiras): about 1500

The Curral das Freiras – which literally translates as "stable of the nuns" – lies in the southern part of the central mountain massif and ranks as one of the most scenically imposing places in the whole of the island. The valley gets its name, as does the village, from the nuns of the convent of Santa Clara in Funchal, who retired here in 1566 after an attack by French pirates.
In the past the almost completely circular Curral das Freiras was thought to be an extinct volcano crater. New research shows, however, that it was much more likely to have been caused by an erosion phenomenon. The river flowing through the valley, on account of its steep gradient, probably ate away at the soft tuff while at the same time sparing the harder basalt stone of the steeply towering rock faces.

Location and importance

From the Eira do Serrado the old, largely cobbled mule track, which until 1959 was the only link between the Curral valley and Funchal, follows a seemingly endless series of bends down to the village of Curral das Freiras. The walk is excellent and takes a good hour.
An alternative is the so-called Lovers' Pass, which begins above Estreito de Câmara de Lobos in the little mountain village of Corticeiras and then leads across the Boca dos Namorados into the Curral das Freiras. For this hike, which requires a certain level of fitness and the appropriate equipment, about four hours should be allowed.

★★Footpaths in the Curral das Freiras

A less demanding method of reaching the village is to take the road, which on the far side of the saddle turns into a series of hairpin bends as it winds its way downwards, passing through a number of tunnels. After 4km it reaches the fertile valley bottom surrounded by high rock faces which is known as Curral das Freiras or Gran Curral. Here on the

Access by car

A layer of thick cloud usually hangs over Curral das Freiras

boulder-strewn bed of the River Ribeira dos Socorridos, which flows into the Atlantic at Câmara de Lobos, is the isolated village of Curral das Freiras.

Sights in the village

★The village

Curral das Freiras was already being used for farming purposes by the nuns of the Convent of Santa Clara before the pirate attack of 1566. The present unassuming little village, situated at a height of 690m, does, however, date from this time. Although cereals, vines and fruit, especially chestnuts, are all grown today, tourism is steadily gaining in importance.

In the 19th c. the nuns had a new church, Nossa Senhora do Livramento, built on the site of the original chapel which was consecrated to St Anthony. The church is in the middle of the village but is generally closed. What is impressive is the grandiose scenery which can be enjoyed by just taking a stroll through the village.

Souvenir shops and cafés line the village square. Specialities which are obtainable here include chestnut, walnut and cherry liqueurs. The little restaurant called Nuns' Valley also serves such unusual dishes as chestnut soup and chestnut cakes.

Eira do Serrado   C 5

Location: 17km north of Funchal
Altitude: 1026m

The road from Funchal to Curral das Freiras (see entry) goes through dense eucalyptus woods and past several viewpoints before reaching Eira do Serrado (Serrado saddle; alt. 1026m) on the north-east edge of the Pico Serrado. Here a road turns off right (1km) to the Miradouro (viewpoint). In the car park there are stalls selling all kinds of souvenirs, as well as more useful things such as hand-knitted cardigans.

Location and importance

A pleasant shaded forest path leads after about 10 minutes' walk to the viewing platform high over the Curral valley. The view from vertiginous heights down into the deep valley bottom (690m), surrounded by steep walls of rock is one of the most marvellous experiences Madeira has to offer.

★★Viewpoint

From the nearby peak of Pico Serrado (literally "sawn-off summit"; alt. 1115m) the visitor will get what is probably the most magnificent view across the whole of Madeira's central mountain chain from **Pico Ruivo de Santana** (1861m) and **Pico de Arieiro** (1818m) in the east to Pico Grande (1607m) and Pico do Jorge (1692m) in the west.

★★Pico Serrado

Around Eira do Serrado there are several well-maintained footpaths which take the walker through a landscape which is at times primeval and totally untouched by man.
  Also recommended is the walk along the centuries-old mule track which leads down into the village of Curral das Freiras (a good hour's walk).

Footpaths

Continue another 3km upwards through mountain scenery full of trees and flowers to the Miradouro Pico dos Barcelos (alt. 355m). The viewing terrace, which is surrounded by a magnificent array of flowers, offers a superb panorama of the south coast of Madeira.

Pico dos Barcelos

Estreito da Calheta   C 2

Location: 65km north-east of Funchal
Altitude: 320–400m
Population: about 3500

The village of Estreito da Calheta is situated just a few kilometres away from Calheta (see entry) and a good 400m higher up. Leaving Calheta on road no. 101 in a westerly direction, after a short distance take the 212 to reach Estreito da Calheta.

Location

Sights

The most important monument in Estreito da Calheta is the Capela dos Reis Magos (Chapel of the Three Kings). Its interior, which was restored just a few years ago, is one of the best examples of the Manueline style of architecture. Of particular interest are the beautiful wooden roof and a triptych made by an unknown 16th c. artist, thought to be from Antwerp. The latter depicts the Three Kings worshipping the child Christ.
  If the chapel is closed, it is possible to obtain the key from the house next door.

★★Capela dos Reis Magos (Chapel of the Three Kings)

Estreito da Câmara de Lobos   C/D 5

Location: 17km west of Funchal
Altitude: 350–500m
Population: about 6000

Location and
importance

Estreito da Câmara de Lobos is situated west of Funchal at a height
of 500m on road no. 214 and is known first and foremost for its
excellent wine. At harvest time each autumn there is a wine festival
lasting several days with folk displays and wine tasting and this has
developed over the years into a tourist attraction. The colourful
bustling Sunday market in the centre of the village is also worth
visiting. Otherwise there are no sights worth mentioning in Estreito
da Câmara de Lobos.

Quinta Jardim
da Serra

From Estreito da Câmara de Lobos a side road leads 4km northwards
to the Quinta Jardim da Serra (alt. 750m) which has a fine view.

★★Cabo Girão

Location

About 4km beyond Estreito da Câmara de Lobos a road branches off
left to the viewpoint overlooking Cabo Girão. The cliffs, which here
drop vertically 589m to the sea, are thought to be the highest in
Europe and the third highest in the world. There is an awe-inspiring
view encompassing a series of terraced fields which seem to grow
ever smaller as they descend. Because they cannot be reached on
foot, intrepid men are lowered on ropes in order to tend them.

The cliffs of Cabo Girão at 589m are the highest anywhere in Europe

Faial

Location: 24km north of Funchal
Altitude: about 150m
Population: about 1500

Beyond Santana (see entry) the coast road keeps to the sea and offers several fine views, until after 7km it reaches the small neat village of Faial (alt. 150m) situated high up over the steep north coast in the middle of fertile gardens of fruit and vegetables; wine production is also commercially important. With its tidily kept houses Faial provides evidence of the prosperity of this area. The village's name is derived from the Portuguese word "faia" (= wax myrtle) and this plant can be found all over the fields.

Location and importance

Sights

The 18th c. church is the destination for a pilgrimage (*romaria*) on September 8th every year.

Village

Both from the square in front of the church and from two viewing terraces up above the village there is a fine vista over the north coast of Madeira with the famous Penha de Águia (eagle rock; 594m), a remote almost cube-shaped rock. There is evidence that ospreys, which had long been thought to have died out on Madeira, are now nesting there. In reasonably clear weather (particularly in the morning) it is possible to make out the promontory of Ponta de São Lourenço (see entry) east of Faial.

Viewpoint

The result of centuries of erosion – Penha de Águia, 594m high

Funchal   D 6

Location: on the south coast of Madeira
Altitude: 2–250m
Population: about 108,000

Location and
importance

Funchal (from "funcho" = fennel), the capital of the archipelago of
Madeira (officially the Região Autônoma da Madeira) and capital of
its own district, is picturesquely situated on the south coast of the
main island of Madeira, amid rich subtropical vegetation.

History

When Henry the Navigator recognised Madeira's advantageous position and its strategic usefulness he sent João Gonçalves Zarco to the
island and the latter first made a settlement at Câmara de Lobos in
1419. In the bay, which was covered with bushes and wild fennel, land
was cleared by burning the vegetation over the course of seven years.
In 1425 Zarco moved his residence to Funchal, from where he admin-
istered that part of the island which had been assigned to him by the
King. In the same year King Manuel II brought together the two feudal
areas of Funchal and Machico and Funchal became the capital.
  By 1500 most of the bay and the valleys leading into it had been
intensively planted with sugar cane using Moorish and black African
slaves. This was to pave the way for the subsequent prosperity of the
island. In exchange for the much sought-after luxury goods that the
island could provide, artistic treasures found their way there and
these now fill Funchal's museums. In the middle of the 16th c, when
the cultivation of sugar cane ceased to be profitable (see Baedeker

Funchal, the capital of Madeira lies in a sheltered bay on the south coast

The Quinta Vigia: one of the many outside Funchal which show evidence of the prosperity of their former owners

Special, p.22), the islanders started producing wine. Funchal became the main trading centre for Madeira wine, which because of shrewd export agreements was shipped not just to Portugal and her overseas territories but also to England and her colonies. Towards the end of the 17th c. more and more English wine merchants had settled in Funchal, including John Blandy (see Famous People), the founder of a wine business which still exists today. The buildings which remain from this time and the magnificent quintas outside the city are proof of the prosperity of their erstwhile owners.

At the same time as mildew and phylloxera inflicted lasting damage on the wine industry in the 19th c., tourism made a cautious start with well-to-do Britons and other Europeans choosing in ever growing numbers to spend the winter on the island. More and more hotels started to be built in Funchal and quintas were turned into guest houses. In the 1970s tourism expanded even more, although along carefully regulated lines. Funchal remains the centre of the Madeiran tourist industry, with by far the majority of hotels on the island being located either in or around the city, particularly on the western side.

Besides being a Roman Catholic diocese, Funchal has a university and a famous hotel management school, as well as possessing the only large harbour in the archipelago. Although often exposed to heavy seas it is an important base for transatlantic traffic. Nowadays, with the completion of the container port at the Caniçal free trade zone, it is used principally as a mooring-place for cruise ships.

In the evenings and at night Funchal offers plenty of variety, with theatres, cinemas, a casino and nightclubs. In one or other of the large hotels there will be some sort of display of folk music or dancing most evenings. On New Year's Eve there is a large firework display to celebrate the New Year.

Funchal

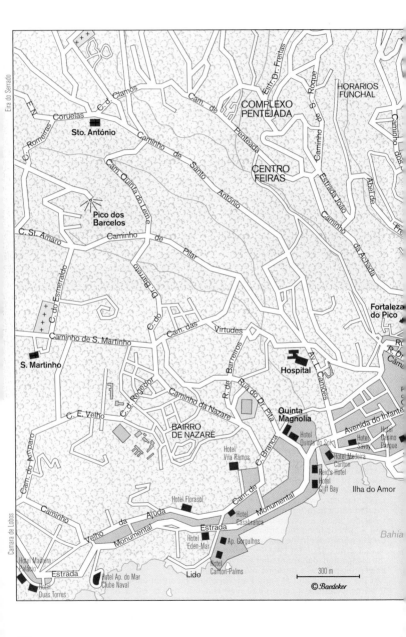

Eira do Serrado

E.N.
C.d. Clamos
Coruelas
C. Romeiras
Sto. António
Cam. de Penteada
COMPLEXO PENTEJADA
Estr. Dr. Freitas
S. Roque
HORARIOS FUNCHAL
Camino dos

Caminho de Santo António
CENTRO FEIRAS
Caminho
Estrada Joao
Abal de
Camino da Achada

Cam. Quinta do Leme
Pico dos Barcelos

C. St. Amaro
Caminho de Pilar

C. do Esmeraldo
C. do Barreiro
C.do
Fortaleza do Pico

Caminho de S. Martinho
Carr. das Virtudes
Av. L. Camoes
R. Dr.
Câma

S. Martinho
R. de Barreiros
Hospital

C. d. Regedor
Rua do Dr. Pita
Quinta Magnolia
Avenida do Infante
Hotel Casino Parque

C. E. Velho
Caminho da Nazaré
Hotel Quinta do Sol
Hotel Savoy

Camino do Amparo
BAIRRO DE NAZARÉ
C. Branca
Hotel Vila Ramos
Hotel Madeira Carlton
Reid's Hotel
Hotel Cliff Bay
Ilha do Amor

Câmara de Lobos
Caminho
da Ajuda
Hotel Florasol
Carr. de Monumental
Estrada
Hotel Casablanca

Velho
Monumental
Hotel Eden-Mar
Ap. Gorgulhos
Bahia

Hotel Madeira Palácio
Estrada
Hotel Duas Torres
Hotel Ap. do Mar Clube Naval
Lido
Hotel Carlton-Palms

300 m

© Baedeker

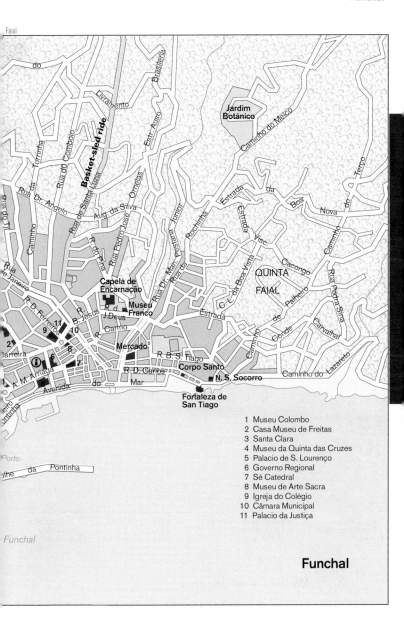

1 Museu Colombo
2 Casa Museu de Freitas
3 Santa Clara
4 Museu da Quinta das Cruzes
5 Palacio de S. Lourenço
6 Governo Regional
7 Sé Catedral
8 Museu de Arte Sacra
9 Igreja do Colégio
10 Câmara Municipal
11 Palacio da Justiça

Funchal

Sights

The steep streets of Funchal, in common with most of the mountain roads on the island, have round, very smooth basalt cobbles and it is therefore best to wear a stout pair of shoes for walking.

The city's unusual geographical position led in the past to considerable transport problems, as the entire east–west traffic for the whole of the southern side of the island was obliged to pass through the narrow streets of Funchal, with no possibility of their being widened. Since the completion of the orbital motorway (1995), above the city to the north, the situation has noticeably improved. Nevertheless there is still a desperate shortage of car parks and it is always advisable to use public transport wherever possible.

★★Cityscape

Funchal is spread out like an amphitheatre across the slopes of a mountain range which rises to a height of 1200m. Even some of the suburbs are situated at heights of as much as 550m. This means that there are spectacular views of the sea from all over the city. The appearance of the city is increasingly becoming dominated by hotel buildings – almost all of Madeira's 12,000 hotel beds are concentrated in Funchal. It has to be said that very few of these hotels attain the style and venerability of Reid's Hotel, which was opened back in 1891 (see Baedeker Special, pp.84–85). Almost all hotels in Funchal, as well as most private houses, are surrounded by carefully tended gardens and parks with a profusion of flowers and greenery.

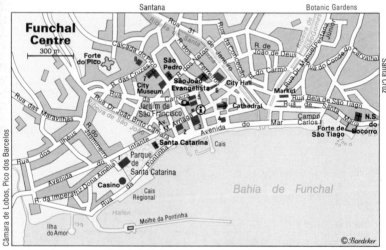

1 Quinta Vigia
(Quinta Angustias)
2 Theatre

3 Palácio de São Lourenço
4 Antiga Alfândega
(Old Customs)

5 Vicente Photographic
Museum
6 Museum of Sacred Art

7 Convent Church
Santa Clara
8 Quinta des Cruzes

Western inner city area

Avenida do Mar
(Promenade)

The magnificent promenade, the Avenida do Mar or Avenida das Comunidades Madeirenses, runs alongside the harbour. Here stands the Palácio de São Lourenço, which was originally built in the 16th c.

The Palácio de São Lourenço built as a fortress for protection against pirates

on the site of an older simple fortification, but subsequently underwent rebuilding on several occasions. The impressive façade overlooking the sea dates from the 18th c. and displays the Portuguese
coat of arms on the east tower. It was the first fortress to be built on
Madeira and is today the residence of the governor and army com-
manders (not open to the public). In the northern part of the governor's palace (access from Avenida Zarco) there is a small permanent
exhibition giving information about the history of the fortress, which
is only occasionally open to the public (at the army's discretion).

On the north-east side of the governor's palace (corner of Avenida
Zarco/Avenida Arriaga) stands a monument in honour of the discoverer of the island, João Gonçalves Zarco. It was built in 1934 by Francisco Franco.

Zarco Monument

In front of the governor's palace a landing stage (Cais da Cidade)
extends out into the sea. It is bordered by the new yachting facilities
and also has many fish restaurants and cafés. What is remarkable
is the graffiti which has been sprayed on the ground and walls by
sailors.

Cais da Cidade

To the north-west, opposite the governor's palace, on the other side of
the Avenida do Dr Manuel de Arriaga is the Jardim de São Francisco.
It was laid out in 1878 on the site of a Franciscan monastery which
was closed in 1834. The gardens are beautifully arranged with an
abundance of palm trees and other tropical plants. In the centre
stands a sculpture of St Francis of Assisi dating from 1982.

★Jardim de
São Francisco
(City gardens)

To the south-east of the Jardim de São Francisco, housed in parts of
the former Franciscan monastery, is the Madeira Wine Company,

★★Madeira Wine
Company

79

which is the oldest and most important wine cellar on Madeira. During the normal opening hours and also at other times for groups by appointment (tel. 223065, fax 227043) there are guided tours, during which explanations are given of the way Madeira wine is produced. There is also the opportunity of sampling and buying wine, including very old vintages, in one of the two tasting bars. One of the bars is named after the German painter Max Romer, who lived on Madeira from 1922 to 1960 and illustrated how Madeira wine is made in a wall painting. A small museum contains old letters and documents as well as historical implements (open: Mon.–Fri. 10.30am–3.30pm; guided tours: Mon.–Fri. 10.30am, Sat. 11am; entry free).

Teatro Municipal

To the south, opposite the Jardim de São Francisco, stands the municipal theatre (Teatro Municipal), built in 1888, in which theatre and cinema performances are held, as well as other communal events and temporary art exhibitions. The small café next door is a favourite meeting-place for young people. To the east, adjoining the theatre, is the building housing the former chamber of commerce. The building, whose extensive façade is decorated with azulejos, dates from the beginning of the 20th c. and is today used as the branch of a Japanese car company.

★★Photographia Museu Vicentes

It is well worth visiting the photography museum "Vicentes", which is situated just to the east of the Jardim São Francisco at Rua de Carreira 43 (open: Mon.–Fri. 2–6.pm, entry charge). On view is the original studio, established by Vicente Gomes da Silva in 1848, which has the distinction of being the first photographic studio in Portugal.

Alongside the original equipment and a large number of old optical and photographical tools there are some albums with highly informa-

The studio of photographer Vicente Gomes da Silva in Funchal

tive historic photographs of Madeira's past. An interesting fact is that there are still a good 350,000 pictures stored in the extensive photographic archive awaiting evaluation. There is a restaurant in the delightful inner courtyard, which dates from the second half of the 19th c.

On the west side of the municipal theatre the Rua do Conselhero José Silvestre Ribeiro leads down to the harbour. On the corner of the Rua das Fontes, looking quite unprepossessing from the outside, is the Casa do Turista, which displays and sells arts and crafts and antiques both from Madeira itself and from the rest of Portugal.

Casa do Turista

Return to the Avenida do Dr Manuel de Arriaga, which continues westwards into the Praça do Infante. The square is named after the "Infante" Henry the Navigator (1394–1460; see Famous People), at whose behest João Gonçalves Zarco took possession of the archipelago in 1420. His monument dating from 1947 adorns the "Rotunda do Infante", which to some extent represents the dividing line between the western area of Funchal and the city centre.

Monument to Henry the Navigator

Henry the Navigator who colonised Madeira

To the south-west, up from the square, stands the small simple Capela Santa Catarina, one of the oldest churches on the island. It dates from the 15th c. and is on the site of an earlier wooden church, which Constança Rodrigues, the wife of the the island's discoverer, João Gonçalves Zarco, had built. The present-day chapel dates from the 17th c. but has since undergone many architectural modifications.

Capela Santa Catarina

Behind the Capela de Santa Catarina lies the Jardim de Santa Catarina, which occupies the site of the former cemetery "Cemitério das Augustas". It today forms a part of the extensive municipal park, which was laid out between 1945 and 1966, and contains several new sculptures, a peacock meadow, parrot enclosures, swan lake and children's playground. The bronze statue "Semeador", which depicts a farmer sowing seeds, is of particular interest.

Jardim de Santa Catarina

The pink-coloured building on the west side of the park is called Quinta Vigia or Quinta das Angústias. While the building today serves as seat and residence of the government of Madeira and therefore cannot be visited, the exceptionally fine park is open daily from 9am to 5pm. The original Quinta Vigia, in which among others the Austrian Empress Elisabeth (popularly known as "Sissi") lived, had to be sacrificed when the Casino Hotel was built.

★Quinta Vigia

Directly next to the Quinta Vigia is the towering round building of the Casino, designed by the Brazilian architect, Oscar Niemeyer. The terrace offers an outstanding view of the city and the harbour.

Casino

To the north of the Jardim de Santa Catarina, on the far side of the Avenida do Infante, stretches the park of the Hospicio da Princesa. The park, which is beautifully looked after, is open to the public. The estate was founded in 1859 by Dona Amelia, the second consort of Pedro I of Brazil, as a hospice for those with lung diseases in memory of her daughter who died from tuberculosis.

★Hospicio da Princesa

The Hospicio da Princesa founded in 1859 by Donã Amelia, the second wife of Pedro I

★★Quinta Magnólia (leisure area)

The Avenida do Infante continues westwards across the steeply descending river course of the Ribeiro Seco and leads to the magnificent 18th c. style parkland of the Quinta Magnólia. Once the seat of the British Country Club, the well-maintained park is now a leisure area open to the public with swimming pool, tennis courts and other sports facilities. The Funchal hotel management school is housed in the estate mansion; there is a restaurant here in which young students of tourism serve an excellent midday meal each day (except Sat., Sun. and holidays).

★Reid's Hotel

To the south-west of the Quinta Magnólia, on the far side of the Estrada Monumental, stands that time-honoured institution, Reid's Hotel (see Baedeker Special, pp.84–85). A visit for five o'clock tea is undoubtedly one of Funchal's main tourist attractions (suitable dress is expected). From the terrace there is a wide view across the city and harbour. The adjoining park with its swimming pool and sea-bathing facilities is reserved for hotel guests.

Hotel area

The Estrada Monumental leads westwards from the Quinta Magnólia and Reid's Hotel out across Madeira's south coast. This is where Funchal's new sprawling hotel district has been established over the last few years. It comprises modern hotels, holiday homes, shopping, sport and leisure facilities.

Walk to the harbour mole of Pontinha

From the west end of the Avenida do Mar the Rua da Pontinha runs south-westwards along the sea and continues below the Parque de Santa Catarina to the old harbour mole of Pontinha, which lies beneath the fortress of Nossa Senhora de Conceição. From the far end of the mole, which was begun in the 18th c. and has been extended several times since then, there is a sweeping view of the whole city.

Eastern inner city area

The harbour promenade to the east of the recently established yacht-ing marina was recently rebuilt. There are several "floating" cafés and restaurants which are pleasant places to visit, including the "Vagrant", a ship which once actually belonged to the Beatles.

Marina (harbour promenade)

On the north side of the Avenida do Mar stands the Old Customs House (Antiga Alfândega). Of the original building dating from 1477 only a small part remains. After being almost totally destroyed in the earthquake of 1748 it was rebuilt later that century and since then has been altered and added to. Only the north doorway survives from the original building and it ranks as one of the finest examples of Manueline architecture on Madeira. The Old Customs House is today the seat of the Regional Parliament (visits on request).

Old Customs House

Only a few hundred metres to the east of the Antiga Alfândega (Old Customs House) is the Praça da Autonomia (Autonomy Square), the central traffic intersection of the city, situated between the outlets into the sea of the two canalized rivers, Ribeira de Santa Luzia and Ribeira de João Gomes. All the main traffic routes from east, west and north meet at this junction.
   In the middle of the square there is a monument commemorating the "Carnation Revolution" and the attainment of autonomy by Madeira in 1974.

Praça da Autonomia

Just north of the Praça da Autonomia is the Largo do Pelourinho with a reproduction of the former city pillory (a fragment of the original is in the Quinta das Cruzes), which was once the symbol of the city's legal jurisdiction.

Largo do Pelourinho

A little way to the north of the Old Customs House there is a pedes-trian precinct dating from the 1980s which gives access to the cathedral, called in Portuguese 'a sé' (from Latin "sedes" = seat (of bishop)). The commission for the cathedral came in 1483 from King Manuel and was given to the master builder, Gil Pedreiro Enes. The cathedral – the first Portuguese one to be built overseas – was com-pleted between 1485 and 1514. The austerity of the building's exterior comes from the contrast between the white plasterwork and the fine Manueline masonry of dark basalt.
   Over the Gothic main portal there is a resplendent rosette, as well as the cross of the Order of Christ, of which King Manuel I was the Grand Master. This cross today forms part of Madeira's flag. The rear façade of the cathedral is also richly decorated with Manueline details. The massive square main tower is crowned by a pyramid-shaped spire covered in geometrically patterned tiles.
   Inside, the cathedral can be described as a triple-aisled basilica. The main altar and the eight side altars, all sumptuously carved and gilded, came from Flanders in the 16th c., along with the choir stalls. They were all paid for with profits from the sugar trade.
   Of special note is the ceiling of the crossing, which is carved from Madeiran cedarwood (actually juniper) and has ivory crustations. It is embellished with ornaments and motives in the Mudéjar style – a style influenced by Muslim artistic elements which the Christianized Moors brought to the Iberian Peninsula.

★★ Sé (Cathedral)

A few hundred metres east of the cathedral there is another fairly recent pedestrian zone which leads to the Largo dos Lavradores and thence to the market hall, the 'Mercado dos Lavradores' (workers' market). The main entrance is decorated with attractive blue and white tiled pictures illustrating activities which take place at the market. Inside, the market stalls are grouped on two levels around a

★★ Mercado dos Lavradores (market hall)

A Cornerstone of the British Empire: Reid's Hotel

As a mere mortal one should approach legends with the appropriate amount of respect – and by that we are not just talking about an attitude of mind but also the external trappings: a visible expression of respect will involve a soberly patterned tie, an equally unobtrusive shirt, a pair of trousers with carefully pressed creases and the very best in leather shoes. Anyone not in tune with this way of thinking will almost invariably catch the strict doorman's beady eye. Smart hotels – and **Reid's Hotel** in Funchal ranks among the most genteel in the world – avail themselves of such liveried attendants at their entrances in order to sort out the wheat from the chaff before entry is granted to the holy of holies. In any case, it is worth a little extra trouble to preserve what must count as one of the last cornerstones of the British Empire. For Reid's is just that; and only the Raffles in Singapore, the Savoy in London and the Peninsula in Hong Kong can really be mentioned in the same breath. Like all of them, Reid's is British through and through, from *The Times* on the breakfast table to the rock-solid institution of five o'clock tea with oven-fresh scones and Earl Grey tea, high above Funchal. And of course there is a separate bridge room! The entrance to Reid's, however, is relatively inconspicuous, so it is as well to pay attention when looking for it in order to avoid driving straight past. Only the curving letters on the brightly polished copper nameplate give any indication of the distinguished address. The narrow driveway is perhaps part of that typically British understatement to which Reid's feels obliged to subscribe, for what is hidden behind this modest entrance can in fact be seen easily enough: as well as the 169 tastefully appointed rooms there are more than 50,000 sq.m of park and gardens with luxuriant subtropical vegetation. Six different types of passion flower alone flourish here, while some of the towering Washingtonia palms and mighty kapok trees date back to the time when the hotel was first built. William Reid, who built the hotel, was born in Kilmarnock in 1822, one of twelve children of a Scottish farmer. When he was 14 he was recommended by a doctor to seek out a warmer climate on account of his poor health. His father, so the story goes, pressed five pounds into the boy's hand and sent him off to find his fortune.

The sickly boy first worked his passage to Lisbon and then on to Funchal, where he found work in a bakery. But soon afterwards he became involved in the wine trade, which was flourishing at this time. Reid became a successful wine-dealer and highly regarded citizen of Madeira, but that did not stop him seeking out new paths to explore. With his wife, Margaret Dewey, he rented out quintas, the gentlemen's houses so characteristic of Madeira, complete with servants and staff. His affluent customers came to Madeira principally because of the pleasant winter climate and would stay on the island for several months. It did not take long before William and Margaret Reid opened their first hotel. With financial support from the then Duke of Edinburgh, the son of Queen

Victoria, Reid bought a quinta and gave it the name "The Royal Edinburgh Hotel". It was the first accommodation on Madeira to be able to boast such a high level of comfort and the success which the leaving it to his two sons William (Willy) and Alfred to open the doors to the first visitors. Further alterations and extensions did nothing to detract from the charm of a hotel with such a special and intimate atmosphere.

The foremost address in Madeira: Reid's Hotel

Reids had encouraged them to build more hotels on the island.

William Reid began the fulfilment of his great dream of a hotel for the rich when he bought a magnificent plot of land with the name Salto do Cavalo (horse's jump). In 1887 building work began under the direction of George Somers, who had already been responsible for designing Shepheard's Hotel in Cairo. Only an extraordinarily gifted architect would have been able to build such a well-appointed building on this bare rock. William Reid did not actually live to see his dream come to fruition. He died just a year after the building work began,

Illustrious guests have always valued these unique qualities and the list of past guests includes George Bernard Shaw, Winston Churchill, Gregory Peck, Roger Moore and numerous members of both the English and European royal families. But it is not just the famous and illustrious who choose to visit Reid's Hotel; there are plenty of others who know how to appreciate its special atmosphere and are perfectly happy to comply with a polite if emphatic request from the management: "You are respectfully asked to wear evening dress after 7 o'clock in the evening."

Funchal Cathedral: simple outside, magnificent inside; the centre of religious life on Madeira

wide, picturesque inner courtyard with trees. Even here the walls are richly decorated with tiled embellishments.

Fruit, vegetables, meat, dairy produce, drinks, flowers, basket and leather ware, and other handmade articles are to be found here, with the largest choice on Fridays and Saturdays when the farmers from the outlying villages come with their goods to sell.

The market building was designed by the Portuguese architect, Edmundo Tavares, in the style typical of the 1930s. Its eastern section houses the fish market, where all kinds of seafood are on sale, including tuna and espada, both at first sight rather unappetizing but at the same time very tasty. It is especially worth coming here in the early morning hours when there is most choice.

★Zona Velha
(old town)

Just to the east of the market hall can be found the old part of Funchal. with its picturesque maze of streets, at present in the process of being restored, its tiny shops, workshops and bars.

To reach the sea go past the Campo Dom Carlos I, the former parade ground, on which a market is held at weekends, and continue eastwards to the Zona Velha, the partly restored former fishing quarter which has a number of good restaurants.

Club Sport
Marítimo

A most unusual museum is to be found on the Rua Dom Carlos Primeiro at no. 14. On the upper floor of the recently renovated building there are some 2200 sporting cups, dating from 1910 to the present day, which have been played for in Portuguese football championships and cup competitions. There are also a large number of pennants and other items which in one way or another are connected with football. In both Portugal and Madeira football is the national

The Mercado dos Lavradores where a large selection of locally grown produce is on sale

game and by far the most popular sport (irregular opening times; entry free).

Right at the start of the Zona Velha on the Largo do Corpo Santo stands the little 16th c. fishermen's church, the Capela do Corpo Santo, which has a few Manueline architectural details.

Capela do Corpo Santo

At the eastern end of the Zona Velha the picturesque Fortaleza de São Tiago guards the tiny bay where the old fishing quarter used to have its harbour. The fort was built in 1614 and dedicated to Saint Jacob the Younger, the patron saint of Funchal. It is open daily and there are particularly fine views from the top storey.

★★Fortaleza de São Tiago

One section of the interior houses the Museu de Arte Comtemporânea (Museum of Contemporary Art). The works displayed are by Portuguese masters of the 20th c. (open: Mon.–Fri. 10am–12.30pm and 2–4pm; entry free).

Underneath the fort is the former fishing harbour, which today is used by locals as a bathing beach, called 'Praia da Barreirinha'.

Praia da Barreirinha

Further north-eastwards past the Fortaleza de São Tiago stands the Igreja des Santa Maria Maior or Igreja de Socorro (Church of the Redeemer), the parish church of the old quarter. Originally built in the 16th c. and consecrated to Saint Jacob the Younger, it was largely destroyed in 1748. The present building, dating from the 18th c., is elaborately decorated with baroque sculptures and carvings. The interior holds the shrine of Saint Jacob the Younger.

Igreja de Santa Maria Maior

Every year on May 1st the Church of Santa Maria Maior is the starting-point for a large procession in memory of the plague of 1538.

Formerly a look-out against pirates, today the Fortaleza de São Tiago houses modern art

Northern inner city area

Praça do Município (city hall square)

North from the cathedral is the Praça do Município, the city hall square, with decorative paving and a fountain. The square is surrounded by houses from the Baroque period, forming an architectural unity. The east side of the square is occupied by the city hall (Câmara Municipal), which was built in 1758 as a stately residence for the Count of Carvalhal and at the end of the 19th c. was designated as the seat of the city administration. The walls of the entrance hall, the staircases and galleries are all decorated with beautiful Baroque tiled pictures. In the picturesque inner courtyard the fountain "Leda with the Swan" is remarkable.

Museu da Cidade (city museum)

The city hall not only houses the administrative offices but also the city museum (Museu da Cidade), which contains noteworthy documents relating to the city's history (open during working hours).

★São João Evangelista (collegiate church)

The north-west side of the Praça do Município is dominated by the collegiate church of São João Evangelista (Igreja do Colégio), which belonged to the former Jesuit monastery. Founded in the 17th c. and run as a seat of advanced learning for boys, it was profaned as a barracks in the 18th c. and is today the seat of the University of Madeira. The façade of the collegiate church is decorated with holy figures; in the interior there are richly gilded carvings and paintings in tiles.

★★Museu de Arte Sacra (museum of sacred art)

The south side of the Praça do Município is taken up by the former Bishop's Palace, dating from the 17th c. Until 1910 it was the seat of the bishop, but since 1955 the building has housed the museum of sacred art (Museu de Arte Sacra; entrance at Rua do Bispo 21). The museum possesses an exceptionally important and interesting collection of Flemish paintings of the 15th and 16th c. These were bought

The Collegiate Church of São João Evangelista – the seat of the University of Madeira

at the behest of rich sugar merchants, which fact alone bears witness to the value of Madeiran sugar at that time, for the paintings are almost entirely from the hands of renowned Flemish painters.

Also worthy of attention are the numerous sacred and profane objets d'art which are of Portuguese origin and date from the 16th –18th c. Particular mention should be made of a collection of liturgical vestments and a mighty processional cross in the Manueline style, made of gold-plated silver, which King Manuel I presented to Funchal Cathedral at the beginning of the 16th c. (open: Tues.–Sat. 10am–12.30pm and 2–6pm; Sun. 10am–1pm; entrance fee, no photography).

From the Praça do Município go first in a westerly direction through the Rua Câmara Pestana and continue upwards to the Church of São Pedro, which dates from the 16th c. Its interior is lined with 17th c. tiles, while the Baroque main altar has copious gold carving. Also of note is the ceiling painted with floral motives.

★Igreja São Pedro

Processional Cross of King Manuel I

Funchal

★Museu Municipal (natural history museum)

Opposite the Church of São Pedro stands the Museu Municipal (municipal museum), actually a natural history museum, which is housed in the 18th c. Palácio de São Pedro. The ground floor has a small aquarium showing sea animals and plants from the waters around Madeira. On the mezzanine there is a library, which is open by appointment (tel. 229761) and on the top floor a collection of fossils and zoological specimens (open: Tue.–Fri. 10am–6pm). Sat, Sun and public holidays, 12 noon–6pm.

★★Casa-Museu Frederico de Freitas

Further up from the municipal museum at the Calçada de Santa Clara stands the former mansion of the Count of Calçada, dating from the 17th c. It now houses the Museu Frederico de Freitas and contains the extensive art and craft collection of the lawyer de Freitas. The rooms of the museum have been fitted out in the authentic styles of various periods, and on display can be seen antique furniture, paintings, ceramics, religious art, as well as everyday utensils and items. The attractive conservatory is also an example of style and taste. Two of the storeys are kept for temporary exhibitions, including those of internationally famous artists (open: Tues.–Sat. 10am–12.30pm and 2–6pm; entry free; partial ban on photography).

★★Convent of Santa Clara

Continuing up the steep Calçada de Santa Clara, on the left stands the Convent of Santa Clara. It was at the end of the 15th c. that the discoverer of Madeira, João Gonçalves Zarco, had the church, a Igreja da Conceição de Cima, built. A little later, between 1492 and 1497, Zarcos' son, João Gonçalves da Câmara founded the convent and had it dedicated to Saint Clara. In the course of time the nuns at the

The cloisters of the former Santa Clara Convent

*The interior of the Convent Church of Santa Clara ▶
contains the mortal remains of Zarco*

convent gained a great deal of influence and the convent acquired a considerable amount of property – not least through donations and bequests. Part of the convent's fortune was derived from the wine trade. When French pirates overran Funchal in 1566 and plundered the convent, the nuns fled to Curral das Freiras (see entry). In the 17th c. there were extensive renovation works and additions to the buildings and these are reflected in the present-day appearance of the convent. While a large part of the original building has fallen victim to modernisation over the years, the Gothic-style north doorway to the adjoining convent church and the convent cloister with its 16th winged altar still remain. Today the Franciscan nuns hold a day centre for needy children in the convent rooms.

Church interior

The side walls of the interior are covered with blue, white and yellow tiles dating from the 16th and 17th c. The choir contains the tomb of the island's discoverer, João Gonçalves Zarco, and those of members of his family. In the rear part of the nave, with its elaborately painted wooden coffer ceiling, it is worth noting the Manueline-style memorial to the son-in-law of Zarcos, Mendes de Vasconcelos.

The convent and church are usually closed to the general public. On ringing the bell at the side door next to the church, permission may be given to see the buildings and sometimes even a free guided tour is given.

★★ Quinta das Cruzes

A little way further up from the Convent of Santa Clara lie the mansion, chapel and park of the Quinta das Cruzes ("house of the crosses"). The estate is said to date back to the 15th c., in other words to the very first period of settlement on Madeira, and is supposed to have been used by João Gonçalves Zarco, the island's discoverer, as a residence. After

The Quinta das Cruzes, a former manor house, now one of the leading museums in Funchal

Largo das Cruzes

Rua das Cruzes

Front Garden

Garden

Orchids

48

Entrance
→

Museu Quinta das Cruzes

© Baedeker

1 Iron Royal Crown
2 Royal Portuguese shield (19th c.)
3 Stoup
4 Dripstone
5 Fragment of a slate tomb
6 Cross (16th c.)
8 Gravestone (1845)
9 Replica of a spring
10 Marble memorial slab
11 Lioz marble memorial slab
12 Memorial slabs (end 15th–beginning 16th c.)
13 Polished gravestone of Belgium stone
14 Gravestone of Madeira Basalt
15 Marble gravestone (1674)
16–17 Memorial slabs of Madeira Basalt
18 Marble stone with family shield
20 Marble stoup
21 Engraved marble stone (1816)
22 Crowned shield and memorial stone (1689)
23–25 Marble fragments
26 Engraved stone (1787)

28–29 Royal Portuguese coat-of-arms
30 Coat-of-arms, stone fragments (18th c.)
31 Coat-of-arms with imaginary shield (18th c.)
32 White marble slab
33 Memorial stone
35 Royal Portuguese shield (18th c.)
36 Fragment of a drinking fountain
37 Carved crown (17–18th c.)
38 Coat-of-arms of the city of Funchal
39 Royal Portuguese shield (17th c.)
40 Stoup
41 Fragment of a memorial slab
43 Shield of the united kingdoms of Portugal,
    Brazil and the Algarve (1816–25)
44 Fragment of a gravestone (16th c.)
46 Engraved memorial slab (1800)
48 Fragment of pillory from Funchal
    (end 15th c.)
49 Small spiral column of white marble
50 Marble shield (1784)
51 Round engraved stone (1726)

being largely destroyed by the earthquake of 1748 it was rebuilt in the late 18th c. using parts of older buildings which were still extant. Since 1953 the Quinta das Cruzes has housed a remarkable museum devoted to the cultural history of the island, which gives an excellent insight into the living conditions of Madeira's more affluent inhabitants from the 16th to the 19th c. Of special interest are the pieces of furniture made from old sugar chests, azulejos, porcelain, silver from the Gulbenkian Foundation and parts of a sunken Dutch sailing ship. Part of the museum is fitted out in the original 19th c. style.

The kitchen of the Quinta das Cruzes with the original 19th c. furnishings

In the otherwise very simple chapel there is an altarpiece by the Portuguese Bento Coelho da Silveira (1618–1708). The mansion of the Quinta das Cruzes is surrounded by a beautifully tended park, famous for its magnificent old trees. Pieces of stonemasonry from the 15th to 19th c. have been set up here, including part of the former city pillory "pelourinho" (there is also a copy on the Largo do Pelourinho), which was ordered to be destroyed as a result of the liberation measures of 1835. Such pillories were not intended in every case to be used for the public humiliation of evildoers; the idea was rather that they should symbolise the city's judicial authority. The fact that the pillory in the garden of the Quinta das Cruzes was mainly of symbolic significance is demonstrated by the elaborate decorations which it bears.

Also of interest are two Manueline windows made from Madeiran basalt (of 1507). They are the last remains of what was probably a very prestigious house in Funchal, of which no more is known, however, than that it was torn down shortly after the turn of the last century (open Tue.–Sat, 10am–12.30pm and 2–6pm).

Fortaleza de São João de Pico

From the Quinta das Cruzes the route continues further north-westwards up through the Calçada do Pico, then left through the Rua do Castelo to the mighty Fortaleza de São João do Pico. Built in the first half of the 17th c. on the Pico das Frias which overlooks the city, it is now used as an army station. As it therefore cannot be entered, the ordinary visitor is denied the wide-ranging view of Funchal which it would provide.

One of the cobbled alleys which are often narrow and steep ▶ in the old town of Funchal

★Cemitério
Británico
(British
cemetery)

To the south-east below the Fortaleza do Pico, running alongside the
Rua do Quebra Costas, is situated the British Cemetery with its Angli-
can church. Both date from the British occupation of Madeira from
1807–14. Until then the burial of non-Catholics and the practice of
non-Catholic beliefs was forbidden on the island.

In the cemetery, alongside the graves of numerous well-to-do citizens of Funchal, stands the family grave of the merchant family of
Blandy (see Famous People).

If the entrance gate to the British Cemetery is closed ring at the neighbouring house and ask for the key.

Surroundings of Funchal

★★Jardim
Botânico da
Madeira
(botanical
gardens)

Situated about 4km north-east of the city centre, the botanical gardens enjoy a prime location with superb views. The site was originally the Quinta de Bom Sucesso, country seat of the Scottish family
of hoteliers, the Reids, and laid out as a private park by them. In 1952
the estate passed into the possession of the city of Funchal, which has
since maintained it as a public park. In different sections of the gardens it is possible to see on display plants native to Madeira, imported tropical and subtropical plants, succulents and more useful
plants (open: daily 9am–6pm; entrance charge).

In the house which was once the Reids' residence there is now a
small, endearingly old-fashioned natural history museum, displaying
animal and plant specimens, as well as fossils found on the island.

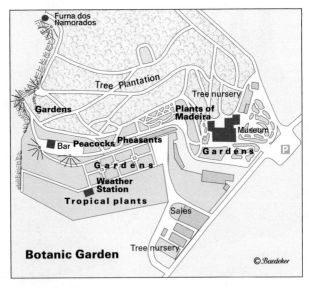

Parrot garden

Directly below the botanical gardens is the Jardim dos Loiros (parrot
garden), which was opened in 1990 and is well worth seeing. Magnifi-
cently coloured parrots from all over the world are on display in spacious aviaries.

Further on, below the parrot garden, in the Rua Pita da Silva is the
orchid garden (Jardim Orquídea), where orchids of all kinds are grown
and sent to other places (opening times as above).

About 10km out of Funchal to the north-east and near the road to Camacha are the extensive grounds of Blandy's Garden (the original Quinta do Palheiro Ferreiro), one of the finest parks in Madeira. In 1790 the Count of Carvalhal had the 12 hectare site fashioned into a

★★ Blandy's Garden

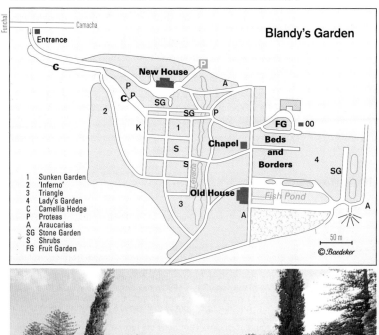

Blandy's Garden

Funchal

Camacha

Entrance

C

New House

P

C P

SG

SG

P

2

K

1

S

S

Chapel

Levada

Old House

3

A

A

P

FG

■ 00

Beds
and
Borders

4

SG

Fish Pond

A

1 Sunken Garden
2 'Inferno'
3 Triangle
4 Lady's Garden
C Camellia Hedge
P Proteas
A Araucarias
SG Stone Garden
S Shrubs
FG Fruit Garden

50 m

© Baedeker

The park of the Blandy family is open to the public; but not the house which is still lived in

garden by a French landscape gardener. His first house with its small baroque chapel lies to the south in the lower part of the grounds. Later the count's nephew had the estate brought more into line with English taste, with an unusually harmonious blend of English and French horticultural traditions resulting. In 1885 the Blandy family bought the property and had a new house built further up, which they still occupy today.

From the main entrance a camellia walk leads to the Blandys' new residence. To the south is the "sunken garden", regularly laid out in the French style and decorated with statues. To the west is the "inferno", an English park with tree ferns, azaleas and rhododendrons. Directly to the east of the estate is the Palheiro Golf Club.

São Martinho   Leaving Funchal in a westerly direction on road no. 101, after about 10km the village of São Martinho (pop. about 2000) can be seen set back from the road. In the church, which dates from the 1930s and 1940s, an 18th c. silver processional cross and various elaborately embroidered vestments are kept. These latter are used on special occasions to decorate holy statues.

Ilhas Desertas   see large map at end of book

Location: about 20km south-east of the main island of Madeira
Altitude: 479m (Deserta Grande), 411m (Ilhéu do Bugio), 104m (Ilhéu Chão)

Access   Boat trips to the Ilhas Desertas (Ilhéu Chão, Deserta Grande and Ilhéu do Bugio) are available in calm seas from Funchal from several tour operators as well as the yachting harbour. Another possibility is to make the journey with the yacht, the "Pirata Azul", which is owned by the office of tourism. Since 1990 it has only been possible for visitors with special written permission to land on the islands. This is normally only granted to people whose reason for visiting has a proper scientific basis.

The island of Deserta Grande is the largest of the three Desertas at 12km long and about one kilometre wide. It is composed of volcanic rock and rises up to 479m above sea level. The name "desert island" is as much as anything due to the lack of water and the consequent barrenness of the soil. In the past there were two attempts to cultivate the islands but these were very quickly abandoned. The same applies to the neighbouring islands of Ilhéu do Bugio and the flatter Ilhéu Chão.

Since 1990 the islands have been placed under a nature conservancy order and as a result are one of the last places of refuge in the world of the rare monk seal (*Monachus monachus*). A small colony now lives here in the sea caves. In addition the highly poisonous Great Wolf Spider (*Geolycosa ingens*) is found here. There is a biological research station on the island of Deserta Grande.

Machico   C 7

Location: 24km north-east of Funchal
Altitude: 2–150m
Population: about 12,000

Location and importance   After the Portela pass, road no. 108 drops down into the delightful Machico valley towards the south coast and after 8km reaches the little fishing port of Machico at the mouth of the Machico river. With about 12,000 inhabitants the town is the second largest settlement on Madeira and presents a picturesque sight with its brightly-coloured fishing boats and small quay. There is also a state-run school for Madeiran embroidery here. The coast is easily accessible here and it is believed that Machico is where João Gonçalves Zarco and his followers first landed in 1419 and founded the first settlement. After Madeira was divided up into an eastern and western part Zarco moved his residence to Funchal in 1440 and entrusted Machico to his companion, Tristão Vaz Teixeira. When Madeira became Portuguese in 1496 and the division of the island was ended, Machico rapidly lost importance to Funchal.

Machico's name is thought to be derived from the Englishman, Robert Machin, who is supposed to have been shipwrecked here when fleeing with his lover, Anne d'Arfet, and therefore can lay claim, from the British point of view at least, to being the real discoverer of Madeira.

Sights

The town centre lies on the west bank of the Machico river. The parish church of Nossa Senhora da Conceição (Our Lady of the Immaculate Conception) was originally Manueline and dates back to the end of the 15th c. The interior was elaborately decorated during the Baroque period with gilded carved woodwork and a painted wooden ceiling. The two portals from Manuel I's time are both preserved; they were a present from the King to the inhabitants of Machico. The left side chapel with the tomb of the Teixeira family also dates from the Manueline period (notice the family's coat of arms over the arch).

★★Nossa Senhora de Conceição

Forte Nossa Senhora do Amparo: once a fortress, today its visitors are treated as guests

Madalena do Mar

Monument to Tristão Vaz Teixeira

In the neat tree-lined church square stands the monument to Tristão Vaz Teixeira.

To the south-east of the parish church stands the second harbour fort from the 17th c. which has still been preserved. The Forte Nossa Senhora do Amparo has a a triangular groundplan and primarily served as a defence against the pirates who constantly plagued Madeira during the 15th–17th c. Today the fort houses the local tourist office.

The western end of the harbour bay was also protected by a fortress, but this had to be demolished when the Hotel Dom Pedro was built.

Capela São Roque

At the western end of the harbour bay stands the tiny Capela São Roque, which was erected in 1489 after a plague epidemic. The chapel was built over a spring which was supposed to work miracles. Inside, the chapel contains some remarkable azulejo paintings which were added in the Baroque style during a complete renovation which took place in 1739. They show scenes from the life of São Roque, who dedicated himself to plague sufferers during an epidemic in Rome in the 14th c. According to the legend, he himself became ill but then is supposed to have been healed by some miraculous means.

★ Fishing quarter

At the eastern end of the harbour bay, to the left of the Ribeira de Machico, is the old fishing quarter, Banda d'Além. It is bounded to the east by the Forte São João Batista, which was erected around 1800 with other fortresses as a protection against pirates.

Capela dos Milagres

In the centre of the fishing quarter, on the Largo dos Milagres, stands the Capela dos Milagres (generally closed). It was built on the site of what was probably the oldest church on the island, which Zarco is said to have had built in 1420 over the grave of the Englishman, Machin, and his lover. After a number of further alterations the chapel was destroyed by a high tide in 1803 and rebuilt in 1815.

A statue of Christ, venerated for its miraculous powers, is kept inside the church. A rogation procession in honour of the statue is held every year on October 8th and 9th. On both evenings bonfires are lit on the mountain slopes around the town.

★ Pico do Facho (Torch mountain)

To the north-east of Machico rises Pico do Facho ("Torch Mountain"). Its name comes from its importance as the location of a watch which had the task of warning the inhabitants of Machico of impending attacks by pirates. Warnings were given by means of enormous bonfires which were lit in the event of a threat and which could be seen far away in Machico. From the top of Pico do Facho there is a marvellous view, which even extends to the cliffs of the Ponta de São Lourenço (see entry).

Madalena do Mar   C 3

Location: 42km west of Funchal
Altitude: 15–120m
Population: about 1500

Location and importance

The coast road from Ponta do Sol (see entry) continues westwards and after a few kilometres arrives at the village of Madalena do Mar. The village is very important historically, because, according to tradition, it was founded by King Wladislaw III of Poland. Although he was officially declared dead after a crushing defeat at the Battle of Warna (1444) against the Turks, it is thought that he survived the massacre and lived on under an assumed name. So the legend goes, he took a vow that he would make a pilgrimage and this led him to Madeira. He is supposed to have been granted vast estates by João Gonçalves Zarco, including what is now Madalena do Mar. The local population called him Henrique Alemão (Henry the German) because of his unknown origins.

It is worth paying a visit to the village church of Santa Catarina, the oldest parts of which are thought to date back to 1457. Downhill from the church stands the house in which King Wladislaw is believed to have lived. It is easily recognised by the coat of arms next to its entrance door.

Monte   C 6

Location: 8km north of Funchal
Altitude: about 450–600m
Population: 9000

Monte is a pretty town with wonderful views, which in the 19th c. and up to the time of the Second World War was a popular health resort with well-to-do Madeirans and with foreigners. Their presence is attested by the large number of imposing houses and villas – called "quintas" – which were generally surrounded by magnificent tropical gardens. Next to them were built several hotels, which ranked among the best on the island. When more recent times saw the shift of tourism to the coastal areas around Funchal, Monte regained its importance as a health resort. However, the venerable old mansions and hotels standing in fine parks, the idyllic fountain square, called the Largo da Fonte, with its former rack-railway station and the Capelinha

Location and importance

The tropical gardens at Monte contain the largest number of species of plants anywhere on Madeira

da Fonte, a tiny chapel always decorated with flowers, are still eloquent reminders of Monte's earlier palmy days.

There are only a few vestiges remaining, however, of one of the technological achievements of that time, the rack-railway, opened in 1893, which went from Funchal to Terreiro da Luta, a difference in height of at least 920m. After a bad steam-boiler explosion in 1930, which claimed several lives, the railway carried on until 1943, when the tracks were dismantled and sold to Portugal and Great Britain. A few surviving bridge arches are the only reminder of the railway today.

Sights

★★Nossa Senhora do Monte

Perched on a mountain ledge above the old village centre of Monte stands the pilgrimage church of Nossa Senhora do Monte. Its curved façade in dark tuff and flanked by two towers, is visible from a considerable distance. Today's church stands on the site of an earlier building, which was built in 1470 by Adam Conçalves Ferreira and consecrated as the Ermida da Incarnação (pilgrimage chapel to the encarnation of the Virgin). It was destroyed in the earthquake of 1748 and completely rebuilt in the Baroque style in 1818. 68 steps lead from the village up to the entrance to the church. The doorway lies underneath a triple-arched arcade and on either side there are notable azulejo decorations. The view from the church terrace across the Bay of Funchal and further south-west to Cabo Girão is superb.

The only remnant of the previous chapel is the small silver pietà in the high altar which is revered by the local population as a patron saint able to work miracles on their behalf. Every year on the feast of the Assumption (August 15th) there is a fair and procession with fireworks (*romaria*) through the streets of the little town.

In the left-hand side chapel is the austere looking sarcophagus containing the mortal remains of Karl of Hapsburg, the last German emperor (see Famous People). He came to Madeira to find a cure for a lung disease and lived for a number of months in the Quinta Gordon, just below Monte and now an annexe of the University of Madeira. Unfortunately the supposedly beneficial climate failed to arrest the progress of his illness and he died in 1922 at the age

A simple sarcophagus contains the remains of Karl von Habsberg

of 34 in the nearby Quinta do Monte. At his own wish he was laid to rest in the church at Monte.

★★Jardim do Monte Palace

On the 7 hectare site of the former Grand Hotel Belmonte, beneath the church at Monte, lies the tropical garden, Jardim do Monte Palace, now owned by the Berardo Foundation for culture, art, technology and science. The park, which has been lovingly and imaginatively laid

A trip in a basket-sled from Monte to Funchal – a highlight of a visit to Madeira

out, has a wealth of artistic details, such as a wall of tiled paintings showing the history of the Portuguese in Japan, a tiled pathway with works from the 15th to 20th c., a collection of porcelain and a museum of mineralogy.

A ride on a "carro de cesta", or basket-sled, from Monte down to Funchal is still a very special experience, notwithstanding the fact that prices have recently risen to such an extent that the trip is beyond the reach of most locals. The sleds are steered by two men who run alongside, so for them it was a real relief when the old cobbles were replaced a few years ago by a proper asphalted roadway. The basket-sled drivers of Monte are required by law to wear their special traditional costumes when on duty.

★★Basket-sled ride to Funchal

It is well worth taking a walk from Monte to Terreiro de Luta, 3km to the north, which is where the old rack-railway from Funchal had its terminus (it is possible to continue the journey on road no. 103). Not far from the old station building, surrounded by superb views, is the 5.5m high statue of Our Lady of Peace (Nossa Senhora da Paz), which stands on a massive basalt pedestal. The construction of the statue goes back to an event which occurred during the First World War, when a German submarine opened fire on and sank a French warship, "Surprise", in the Bay of Funchal. Afterwards the Madeirans vowed to erect a monument to the Virgin Mary when the war was finally over. Contributions from every conceivable source ensured that the promise was fulfilled in 1927. A rosary made from the anchor chain of the sunken warship is wound round the pedestal.

Walk to Terreiro de Luta

Beyond Terreiro de Luta the 103 continues upwards into the mountains and after another 6km reaches the top of the pass at Pico Poiso

Trip to Pico Poiso

(alt. 1412m). A good-quality road branches off left here and for the next 7km passes through scenery which is wooded at first, but later turns into moorland and finally becomes rugged and mountainous with breathtaking views. The road finally reaches the car park next to the Pousada of Pico do Arieiro (alt. 1818m), the third highest summit on the island. From the various terraces the visitor can enjoy the magnificent panorama across the central mountain range of Madeira.

A simple footpath leads from the pousada down to the Miradouro do Juncal (1800m), which affords an extensive view of the island's north coast.

Paúl da Serra (High plateau)   B/C 3–4

Location: about 60km north-west of Funchal
Altitude: 1300–1400m

Location and importance

The misty plateau of Paúl da Serra (= mountain swamp) lies at a height of 1300–1400m and extends over an area of 102sq.km, making it the only real area of flat land on Madeira. This wilderness, with its large numbers of sheep and goats living wild, in many ways resembles the Highlands of Scotland and is in marked contrast to the rest of Madeira with its picturesque profusion of flowers and scenic variety. The highest point in the area is the Ruivo do Paúl (alt. 1640m), while there is a fine viewpoint on the Campo Grande (Bica da Cana, 1620m), with a government-run inn.

The plateau of Paúl da Serra is very important for the island's water supply. The porous stone is actually like an enormous sponge which soaks up the precipitation which it receives. The water then flows downhill either as streams or in the numerous levadas which start around

Wild sheep on the plateau Paúl da Serra

The dead-straight road 204 leading to the Paúl da Serra plateau

here. The only real landmarks in the otherwise bleak landscape of the Paúl da Serra are the three dozen or so wind turbines which were erected in 1993 and are used for the production of electricity. It is planned that their number will be further increased.

On the other hand, the idea of establishing Madeira's new airport on the Paúl da Serra, because of its favourable geographical conditions, in the end proved a non-starter. The plan was abandoned because of the unpredictable visibility to which the plateau is subject.

The plateau is almost devoid of people except in June each year when the sheepshearing festival is held. The sheep are rounded up and shorn and the whole operation takes on the character of a great popular festival. To find the exact date of the festival make enquiries in the tourist information office in Funchal.

★Sheepshearing festival

The road which crosses the Paúl da Serra has several viewpoints and is also a good starting place for walkers who wish to explore the high mountain areas. Even for the less experienced or energetic walker there are some very rewarding paths.

★Mountain walks

One of these recommended walks begins about 9km north of Canhas at the statue of Christ, known as Cristo Rei. From here the walk follows the Levada do Paúl, which crosses many tiny hills and humps. In fine weather the water glistens causing an optical illusion: it is as if the water is flowing uphill. If the path is followed further, there are several viewpoints. On the right-hand side the path overlooks the plateau, while on the left there is a view down towards the south-western coast of Madeira. Other landmarks are two small waterfalls, some pools and caves. The levada flows into a reservoir which supplies the water-power station at Calheta (see entry).

Walk along the Levada do Paúl

Levadas:
Water for Everyone

One of man's greatest achievements on the island of Madeira is the elaborate irrigation system, known as **levadas**. And with a total length of 2150km it must be the longest man-made canal network in the world.

The construction of the first levadas dates back to the time of the first settlement on Madeira. The men who under João Gonçalves Zarco cleared large tracts of primeval forest by burning and then cultivated the land were faced with the difficulty of finding an adequate water supply. But in identifying this problem they were quick to notice a consequence of the marked seasonal variation in climatic conditions: while on the damper northern side of the island there was frequent rainfall and therefore water in abundance, the much sunnier southern side was extremely dry. History has not recorded who first had the idea of building the first levadas (the Portuguese verb "levare" means "to carry"). What is certain is that slaves were abducted from Africa and brought to Madeira to sweat blood laying the first canals on the island. The biggest obstacle for the canal builders was the topographical conditions. Every stone, every tool used had to be physically carried to wherever the planners had decided on as the best course for the levada to follow.

Today the levadas are still supplied with water from natural springs or from large reservoirs which ensure an even flow. Before the water reaches the banana plantations, the vegetable fields and the vineyards, it will have fulfilled a second purpose – notably that of producing electricity, for a far from insignificant proportion of Madeira's energy needs are today met

by hydro-electric power and it is envisaged that this use can be maximised further.

In order to avoid dissension among farmers and distribute the water supply as equitably as possible a special levada law was passed quite early on. From the beginning the authorities took control and granted to all interested parties the licence to take their allotted amount of water. In order to prevent disputes the government appointed supervisors, called "heréus". These men were not only in charge of the distribution of the water, but also had the task of maintaining the levada network.

Today their successors are known as "levadeiros". They are paid out of public funds and carry out the often demanding job of keeping the complicated canal system in order. They are each responsible for a specific section of canal and have to clear it of any waste which gets caught in the special grilles. In order for them to be able to do this there is a narrow path running alongside each levada, which not only passes through public land but also crosses private property. The levadeiro has the right to go anywhere at any time, including on private land, in order to carry out his job of maintaining the levada. In addition the landowner has always had to relinquish the right to assume exclusive use of any water source occurring on his property. In return the government guarantees that it will levy no charges for water supplied from the levadas and will meet the costs of upkeep.

There are still some levadas in use today which date back to the 15th and 16th c., but by far the largest part of the present-day network was laid during this century. For a number of years now, however, no new levadas have been built, the last important one being the Levada dos Tornos in 1966. Its course follows the south-facing mountain slopes above Funchal and irrigates land over a length of

for varied and fascinating walks through wonderful scenery using the paths running alongside the levadas. But not every levada is suitable for just any walker. Some of the paths should only be tackled by those experienced in mountain walking and

Walks along the levadas is one of the nicest pastimes in Madeira

more than 100km, with more than 10,000 outlets supplying water to an area in excess of 10,000 hectares. Since the 1950s, following a period when a rather futile privatisation of the canal system was attempted, there has again been a state commission which supervises the levada network and maintains a rolling programme of modernisation.

The levadas also serve other purposes, one of which is as a means of transportation for goods of all kinds. Then, in the present century, nature-lovers and others visiting Madeira realised that they could go

used to heights. Such levadas follow steep rock faces and the width of the paths is such that the greatest possible care should be taken. Inexperienced ramblers and possibly those not adequately equipped or dressed are likely to be in consider-able danger. They are better advised to undertake one of the many less demanding levada walks which still pass through almost equally impressive scenery. For example, the Levada dos Tornos which passes through green and luxuriant garden scenery overlooking the Bay of Funchal.

Pico de Arieiro   C 5

Location: 25km north of Funchal
Altitude (summit): 1818m

Location and
importance

Pico de Arieiro is the third highest mountain on Madeira – and also the one that is the most accessible. A well-maintained road actually ends just a few metres below the summit, so that the distance from Funchal can be quickly covered in about an hour. Along this road there are several viewpoints which offer magnificent panoramas of the island if the weather is reasonably clear.

On the plateau near the summit there is a hotel with a small restaurant and of course the inevitable souvenir sellers. What is unusual, however, is an unprepossessing building which was built about 1800 and was used as an icehouse. Snow, which falls on Pico de Arieiro from time to time, used to be pressed together, stored and then sold to the hotels in Funchal.

Note
For the trip to Pico de Arieiro it is advisable to choose the early morning hours or to spend the previous night in the well-appointed pousada, as even by late morning the view is usually considerably restricted by the build-up of cloud. In case of doubt, it is a good idea to consult the local weather forecast, assuming some knowledge of Portuguese.

★★ Walk to
Pico Ruivo

The walk from Pico de Arieiro to Pico Ruivo de Santana (1861m), the highest mountain on Madeira, takes about four hours. It is very rewarding, but requires staying power and the right equipment (stout shoes, warm waterproof clothing, a torch and food). From the summit one's effort is rewarded by a superb view of the island!

From the summit of the Pico de Arieiro the three highest mountains in Madeira are a breathtaking sight

Pico Ruivo de Santana (mountain)   B 5

Location: about 45km north of Funchal
Altitude (summit): 1861m

With a height of 1861m Pico Ruivo de Santana (generally just known as Pico Ruivo) is the highest point on Madeira. Even when lower-lying areas of the island are shrouded in thick mist, the mountain's steep red-tinged peaks are likely to be visible in clear sunshine. Climbing to the summit of Pico Ruivo will therefore let the visitor see for himself the fascinating diversity of Madeira's weather patterns. *Location*

An ascent of Pico Ruivo begins at the Achada do Teixeira, where road no. 202 ends (Beware: the last section of the road is chained off after sunset!). It is possible to arrange to be driven out here from Funchal and brought home again; there are a few parking places for hired cars. The ascent does not demand any special level of fitness, but it is advisable – as on any mountain expedition on Madeira – to have solid footwear with a good grip and clothing appropriate to the type of weather liable to be encountered. About two hours should be allowed for the climb up and back again. *★★Ascent of Pico Ruivo*

From the car park looking to the north it is possible to make out an imposing basalt rock formation which looks like someone standing and is therefore popularly known as Homem em Pé (man standing). The well-made footpath makes its way up numerous steps and levels to a height of 1640m, where there is a refuge hut for a rest. Even here there is a wonderful view across the majestic landscape of the central mountain massif. Of particular interest is the varied geological structure which can be discerned. The ascent goes past another two huts and several superb viewpoints before arriving at the summit.

Pico Ruivo de Santana gets its name from the shining red clay of the area

Ponta Delgada   B 5

Location: about 60km north of Funchal
Altitude: about 10–165m
Population: 2500

Location and
importance

The village of Ponta Delgada lies on the north coast of Madeira on a small promontory. It is famous for its naturally formed swimming pools in the rock which the surf keeps filled with fresh sea-water. Fruit and vegetable growing are important here, and many of the willow canes which are used by Madeira's basket-makers come from here.

Feast of the
wooden crucifix

One of the oldest religious festivals on Madeira takes place every year in Ponta Delgada on the first Sunday in September. It commemorates a legend according to which in 1470 a chest containing a wooden crucifix was washed ashore – just at the time when a small chapel was built and therefore named Capela do Senhor Bom Jesus. In later times the chapel was rebuilt on several occasions and extended, but in 1908 it was almost completely burnt. Only the charred remains of the cross were spared and, since the church was rebuilt in 1919, this has been stored in a glass container. It is still much venerated by the local faithful.

Ponta de São Lourenço Peninsula   C 8–9

Location: 34km east of Funchal
Altitude: 0–322m

Location and
importance

Road EN 101–3 leaves Machico in a northerly direction and first skirts round the Pico do Facho (see Machico), which dominates the whole of the harbour bay. From here the arrival of ships was signalled by beacons, while today the summit affords a fine panoramic view.
   The Ponta de São Lourenço is reached via a 750m long road tunnel which was built in 1956 and has more recently undergone improvements. An arresting impression is created by the arid landscape through which the road subsequently passes as it continues along the promontory marking Madeira's easternmost limit. The scenery resembles a desert; in summer the orange-red stone appears very dramatic, with only the occasional withered bush or cluster of particularly hardy plants, such as thistles. In winter, however, and also in spring, when there are heavy showers even here, the deserted boulder-strewn landscape is transformed into a verdant and blooming terrain where sheep and goats and even cows graze. To that extent the climate on the peninsula is more like that on the neighbouring island of Porto Santo than the rest of Madeira.

★★Circular trip
across the
peninsula

The road ends at the car park of Ponta do Buraco high above the Abra bay. From here there is a rewarding walk on footpaths through really impressive scenery. For safety reasons it should not be attempted in misty weather.

The scenery of the peninsula of Ponta de São Lourenço ▶
changes dramatically with the changing seasons

Ponta do Pargo

From the bay the view extends from north to south right across the almost vertical cliffs which plunge down to the sea. In the north-east it is possible to make out the neighbouring island of Porto Santo (see entry) and the Ilhas Desertas (see entry) to the south-east.

On the top of the mountain crest which runs along the length of the peninsula can be seen a series of wind turbines which supply electricity to the recently established industrial and free-trade zone of Caniçal.

Footpaths

From the car park there are several other easy footpaths leading to good vantage points, some of them with even more remarkable views. One extremely rewarding walk (stout shoes, experience of mountain walking and a supply of water absolutely essential) leads down to the Abra bay (4hrs there and back). There, surrounded by palm-trees, stands the deserted Casa da Sardinha with its small jetty and good places to bathe. From here it is another hour's walk to the Ponta do Furado, a prominent lava rock. Here there is also an excellent view of the coastal cliffs of Madeira and across to Porto Santo and the Desertas.

Ihéu de Agostinho/Ilhéu de Farol

Lying offshore from the Ponta do Furado are the uninhabited islands of Ilhéu de Agostinho and Ilhéu de Farol with its lighthouse built in 1870, which marks the easternmost point on Madeira.

Ponta do Pargo   B 1

Location: 79km west of Funchal
Altitude: 473m
Population: about 3000

Location and importance

The little country town of Ponta do Pargo, the most westerly locality on the island of Madeira, serves an area which is one of the richest in tradition. This adherence to the past is illustrated by the fact that this is almost the only place where the inhabitants still don the beautiful old traditional costumes on public holidays. The name of the village means "place of the dolphins".

Sights

Festa do Pero (apple festival)

Once a year the otherwise rather sleepy place comes to life, when in September the apple festival, a Festa do Pero, is held. It goes without saying that the inhabitants really enjoy putting on their colourful traditional costumes for this event.

Lighthouse

While the village itself has no sights of any interest, there is a single-track road which leads to the lighthouse (392m) which marks the most westerly point on Madeira. From here there is a good view across the western tip of the island.

Another footpath leads from the village down to the Praia do Pesqueiro, the fisherman's beach, surrounded by cliffs.

Walk along the Levada Nova

There is an excellent walk from Ponta do Pargo to Calheta (see entry) along the Levada Nova. The walk is about 21km along, but the course of the levada is never very far from road no. 101, where there are bus-stops. The effort is well worth while as there is an extraordinary variety of wild flowers and plants to be seen along the route.

Ponta do Sol

C 3

Location: 42km west of Funchal
Altitude: about 30–180m
Population: about 4500

The name of the little town of Ponta do Sol on the south coast of Madeira means something like "place in the sun", which can be attributed to the fact that the rocks which surround the village do not cast any shadows. The village, which was founded in 1450 and received a town charter in 1501, was once the centre of sugar cane growing on Madeira. Today it is surrounded by extensive banana plantations and has one of the largest banana packing stations. The fruit is then transported to Funchal by lorry before being exported abroad. In the middle of the 19th c. a quay for ships was built which still exists. Hopes that there would be a tourist boom in Ponta do Sol have only partially been realised, although the town is a popular stopping place for almost all the organised tours around the island.

Location and importance

Ponta do Sol was the birthplace of the grandfather of the famous American novelist, John Roderigo dos Passos (1896–1970), who achieved world renown wih his works "42nd Parallel" and "Manhattan Transfer", breaking through the forms of traditional realism. His grandfather left Madeira in the 19th c. and emigrated to the United States. The grandson visited his grandfather's home several times, the last visit being in 1960 (a plaque on his former home in Rua Príncipe D. Luís I commemorates this event, which the inhabitants of Ponta do Sol still talk about with pride).

The harbour promenade at Ponta do Sol with its little pavilion – a good place for a coffee break

Sights

The best view of Ponta do Sol is from above the town from the road which winds its way down into the valley. At the harbour there is a well-kept promenade; of note is the small wrought-iron pavilion with an elaborately decorated pointed roof.

★★Nossa
Senhora
da Luz

The Church of Nossa Senhora da Luz (Our Lady of the Light) is situated on the site of an earlier building which was erected back in the 15th c. and is thought to have been one of the oldest religious buildings on Madeira. Later the church underwent fundamental alterations on several occasions, most notably in the 18th c. Only a statue of the patron saint and a font, thought to have been donated by King Manuel I himself, are preserved from the original building. The most comprehensive alterations occurred in the 18th c., when it was redecorated in the Baroque style with magnificent colours and beautiful details. The original wooden ceiling in the choir was retained, but repainted in the Baroque style.

★Quinta da
João Esmeraldo

Situated about 2km above Ponta do Sol, in the village of Lombada, surrounded by extensive banana plantations, is the Quinta of João Esmeraldo. It was built by a companion of Christopher Columbus who in the 15th c. managed the largest sugar cane plantations on Madeira and employed many hundreds of slaves. The quinta, which is said to have been visited by Christopher Columbus, today belongs to the regional government and, following major restoration, is now used as a school. The chapel of Espírito Santo, which forms part of the estate, was renovated in the 18th c. and decorated with beautiful wood carvings and azulejo tiles.

Porto Moniz   A 3

Location: 42km north of Funchal
Altitude: about 10–280m
Population: about 2500

Location and
importance

The village of Porto Moniz lies at the north-western tip of the island. Before the coast road arrives at the village it has to make numerous hairpin bends as it winds its way down to the sea. Not least because the only campsite on the whole of Madeira is located at Porto Moniz, the fishing village is a favoured summer resort, even among Madeirans. It owes its name to Francisco Moniz, who settled here in 1533 in order to administer his estates.

Thanks to a promontory which protrudes a long way out to sea and the offshore island of Ilhéu Mole, with its fishermen's houses, lighthouse and small fortress, Porto Moniz has the best protected and most important harbour on the north coast of Madeira and was a whaling station for a number of years.

Sights

One important visual characteristic of Porto Moniz is the way that the fragile vines are protected against the occasional gale-force winds. At the harbour the remains of a small fort are still visible. It was built in the 17th c. to ward off attacks by pirates.

Porto Moniz is also famous for its restaurants in which delicious fish dishes are served.

Porto Moniz, in the north-west of Madeira, is a popular summer holiday resort

To the west of the harbour mole the powerful rugged coastline forms numerous natural water pools, which are connected one to another by artificial channels. In suitable weather it is possible to have a refreshing bathe here.

★Natural swimming pools

Beyond Porto Moniz the road continues close to the sea along the north coast of Madeira in an easterly direction. It is often cut deep into the cliffs and is not only impressive in engineering terms but also exciting, often becoming just one lane through tunnels, as well as passing underneath waterfalls. There are magnificent views of the cliffs along Madeira's north coast. The damp rock faces are ideal for flat-growing flowers and plants.

★★Continuing along the north coast

Porto Santo
(see large map at end of book)

Location: 43km north-east of the main island of Madeira
Altitude: 0–517m

The table-shaped island of Porto Santo is surrounded by five small reef islands and lies at 32° 59′40″N and 16° 16′35″E about 43km north-east of Madeira. The island is about 11km long and 6km wide with an area of 42.5sq.km and its highest point is Pico Facho (517m). There are about 5000 people living on Porto Santo, who earn a livelihood principally from fishing, but more recently from tourism as well. The sandy beach, stretching for over 9km is extremely popular, particularly in the summer holiday season when it is a favourite holiday destination of families from the main island of Madeira. Porto Santo's economy also depends on the NATO airbase established in the 1960s.

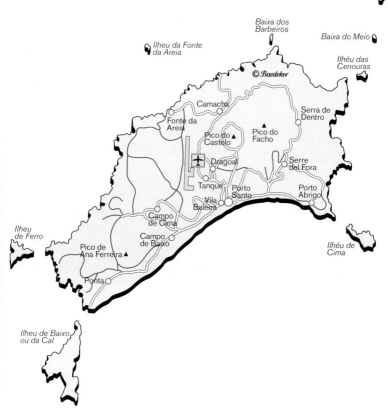

History

It is a historical fact that João Gonçalves Zarco, Tristão Teixeira and Bartolomeu Perestrelo came upon the Madeiran archipelago in 1418. Before they landed on Madeira itself they first established themselves on the more easily accessible island of Porto Santo, in order to assess the possibility of making a settlement on the main island. On Porto Santo they found a wooded island covered with dragon trees, juniper and scrubland.

In 1420 Perestrelo returned to the island with Portuguese settlers, mainly from the Algarve and Alentejo, and began to make it cultivable. In the annals it is noted that a pregnant rabbit which had been set loose by the discoverers in 1418 had in the intervening two years multiplied to such an extent that the plague of rabbits represented a real problem for the newcomers in the first few years.

The most famous inhabitant of Porto Santo was, however, the sailor and discoverer, Christopher Columbus (see Famous People), who spent several years on the island around 1450. Here he married Filipa Moniz, Perestrelo's daughter, and is supposed to have conceived the first definite ideas for his later voyages of discovery. The house where he lived is in Vila Baleira and today houses a small museum.

Porto Santo offers a very different landscape from Madeira – it has few streams and consequently little water

In the 15th c. and through to the 18th c. Porto Santo suffered greatly from raids by Moorish, French and English pirates. In order to protect the island from these attacks a small fort was built on the top of Pico Facho. Nothing remains of the fort today.

The climate is very even and means that a bathe in the sea is possible all the year round. There are also a number of mineral springs, the waters from which are supposed to help people with rheumatism, calcium deficiency and other medical conditions.

Climate

There is a daily boat connection between Maderia and Porto Santo★; the crossing lasts about 3 hours. In addition there are several daily flight connections to Porto Santo fron Santa Catarina Airport on Maderia (tuboprop planes; flight time: 20 mins).

Access

★ There are regular boat services from Funchal to Porto Santo with Porto Santo Line, Rua da Praia, Funchal Tel. 226511 Fax. 232758.

Porto Santo offers the visitor a completely contrasting landscape to that of Maderia. The sandy heights of the island, coupled with its intense aridity, explained by the lack of rivers and water sources, means that the 5000 inhabitants can cultivate the land only with the greatest of difficulty (grain, wine, fruit and vegetables). Windmills are a feature of the landscape, while cattle graze on the open pastureland.

Landscape

Sights

The main town and harbour of Vila Baleira is situated on the south coast of the island. By far the majority of the population live here.

Vila Baleira

Porto Santo

Nossa Senhora da Piedade

The simple parish church of Nossa Senhora da Piedade stands on Largo do Pelourinho on the site of a former chapel dating from 1420 and 1446. The church was rebuilt in 1667 after being laid waste and pillaged by pirates. Only a few fragments of Gothic vaulting remain from the previous building.

Town hall

The town hall (Câmara Municipal) of Vila Baleira is also situated on Largo do Pelourinho and is a good example of Portuguese renaissance architecture. It dates from the late 16th c., but has undergone various later alterations.

★★Casa de Colombo (Columbus's house)

The house in which Columbus is supposed to have lived is today a small museum with all sorts of tools and implements from the everyday life of that time, as well as old maps, charts, pictures and documents relating to the history of seafaring (open: daily except Sun. and public holidays 9.30am–noon, 2.30–5pm; entrance charge). Sat. 10–noon.

Capela Nossa Senhora da Graça

About 1500m east of Vila Baleira stands the Capela Nossa Senhora da Graça, which is much revered by the local people for the healing powers of its spring. It occupies the site of an earlier 15th c. chapel which was destroyed in 1812 and for a long time lay in ruins. The present-day building dates from 1951.

Portela viewpoint

Nearby is the Portela viewpoint, from where there is a good vista of the south of the island including the Ilhéu de Cima (lighthouse).

★★Campo de Baixo (sandy beach)

In contrast to the main island of Madeira, Porto Santo possesses a wide beautiful sandy beach which stretches for a length of 9km along the south coast. There are also a number of small sandy bays else-

The 9km-long beach at Campo de Baixo is Porto Santo's biggest asset

where, tucked away on the steep rocky sections of coast. Facilities for tourists are starting to be established.

To the north-east, above Vila Baleira, rises the tree-covered Pico do Castelo (437m), the cone of a long extinct volcano. On its summit stand the sparse remains of a 16th c. fortress. From here there is a fine view over the north of the island.

Pico do Castelo

Further east lies the summit of Pico Facho (517m; viewpoint), the highest point on the island and also of volcanic origin. Nothing remains of the fortress which once stood here.

★Pico Facho

In the area between Vila Baleira and the airport a national park has been established in the last few years as a result of extensive afforestation.

National Park of Porto Santo

The west of the island is dominated by Pico de Ana Ferreira (283m) with its interesting basalt column formations. On its southern slope stands the Capela de São Pedro (17th/18th c.), which is only open to the public once a year on St Peter's Day (June 29th).

Pico de Ana Ferreira

From Ponta da Calheta, the south-west tip of Porto Santo, there is a fine view across to the little offshore island, Ilhéu de Baixo, as well as Madeira and the Desertas. Both restaurants here serve excellent fish dishes.

Ponta da Calheta

On the steep north coast of the island, surrounded by bizarre rock formations, can be found the "Fonte de Areia", a mineral spring which was set in stone in 1843. Its water, supposedly the source of eternal youth, is bottled and exported to Madeira and Portugal.

Fonta da Areia (mineral spring)

Rabaçal   B 3

Location: 65km north-west of Funchal
Altitude: 1064m
Population: about 200

Rabaçal is situated amid truly breathtaking scenery on the road which crosses the high plateau of Paúl da Serra (see entry). The little village is surrounded by woodland consisting of laurels and tree heath, alternating with a rich variety of ferns, mosses and lichen. Even the most seasoned of travellers are likely to be captivated by scenery such as this. The actual village of Rabaçal lies in a well-defined valley and comprises just a few inns run by the government. The area around Rabaçal is a popular destination for people on weekend outings as there are a number of excellent picnic spots. The name of the village means "unspoilt" or "virginal" and could equally well apply to the whole of the surrounding scenery.

Location and importance

Rabaçal is not served by public transport. It is possible to take a taxi to the starting-point of the walks and strolls described below. Those driving on their own should use road no. 204 and should be aware that maximum care is needed in negotiating the road up the valley to Rabaçal. The narrow road goes past steep drops in several places and there are no protective barriers. It is usual, in the event of two cars meeting on this road, for the one going uphill to reverse back to the first available passing place and let the oncoming vehicle come past.

One of the many beautiful footpaths around Rabaçal with a natural "roof" of tree branches

Sights

★★Landscape

The car park at Rabaçal is both the end of the road and a wonderful starting-point for short strolls and longer walks. More of a stroll than a walk is the path to the Vinte e Cinco Fontes (25 springs), which can be reached in just a quarter of an hour. Several streams pour into a pool, some of them over tiny waterfalls. The amount of water in the pool varies according to the time of year. This highly picturesque little lake supplies water to the Levada do Risco.

Walk along the Levada do Risco

A magnificent walk, and one that is relatively easy, goes from the Rabaçal car park and follows the Levada do Risco to the waterfalls of the same name. These cataracts are among the most spectacular on Madeira. The path begins at the car park in Rabaçal and from here follow the sign saying "Risco", not the path to Vinte e Cinco Fontes. The walk only takes about half an hour but for nature lovers it offers a wealth of sights and sounds. At the end of the path there is a small marked-off area with tables and benches. Forming a backdrop for this picnic spot are the two waterfalls which plunge close to one another over a drop of more than 100m into the deep.

Walk along the Levada da Rocha Vermelha

Another walk, which does not pose any great problems in terms of fitness or foothold, is the one which follows the Levada da Rocha Vermelha. For reasons of safety, however, it is not advisable to do it either when it is raining or immediately after a fall of rain. Even at other times the stones can be slippery and firm footwear is essential. The levada was only laid in 1969 and therefore is one of the newest on Madeira. The walk is on a path which follows the winding course of the levada. At various points along the route there are views of lush green valleys and mountain slopes. One of the best of these views is the one down into the deeply indented valley of the little River Janela.

Ribeira Brava   D 4

Location: 32km west of Funchal
Altitude: about 30–180m
Population: about 7500

Ribeira Brava is a little fishing town at the mouth of the stream bearing the same name (it means "wild stream") situated on the southwest coast of Madeira.

The town is one of the oldest settlements on the island. Part of its importance can be ascribed to its location at the intersection of some key routes across the island. Merchants and traders, when travelling around the island, would meet here in order to conclude business deals. With the opening up of the transport network, which worked to Ribeira Brava's advantage, a certain prosperity came to the village. In the future it is expected that the town, with its convenient position and all year round pleasant climate, will see a steady increase in tourism.

Location and importance

Sights

The neat and tidy impression which Ribeira Brava gives doubtless comes from the quiet prosperity which its inhabitants enjoy. A walk around the little town, which need not take more than half an hour, will yield a number of attractive examples and features of typical Madeiran architecture: brightly-coloured window shutters, wrought-iron balcony rails and divided façades.

Townscape

The Igreja São Bento is one of the last well-kept examples of Manueline architecture on Madeira

Ribeira da Janela

A small fort dating from the 17th c. stands just above the bank of the stream. Every year at the end of June the picturesque "Festas de São Pedro" are held here with a procession and folk music and dance demonstrations.

Breakwaters were once built along the rough shingle beach but they achieved their purpose for only a very limited length of time. The force of the sea caused the part of the breakwater lying under the water to be gnawed away to such an extent that it has even been suggested that the ugly concrete monstrosities should be demolished.

On the promenade by the shore the remains of an old fort can be seen. It was constructed in the 17th c. to offer protection against pirate attacks.

★Igreja São Bento

In the town centre not far from the harbour, on a square with pebble mosaics, stands the Igreja São Bento, a charming village church dating from the 16th c. The top of the tower is decorated with blue and white tiles. Inside there is a font which was a gift from King Manuel I in about 1500.

In addition the Manueline-style chancel, the magnificent Baroque altar, installed at a later date, and some artistic azulejos are all worthy of note.

Town hall

Only a few metres from the church stands the town hall of Ribeira Brava, which is housed in a gentleman's house dating from 1776 (the same date is found inscribed over the entrance portal). Attached to the building are superb gardens, almost like a park, which are open to the public.

Continuing on to São Vicente

The road to São Vicente leaves Ribeira Brava in a northerly direction and climbs up inland, mostly following the west side of the course of the Ribeira Brava. The route passes through some marvellous scenery.

Ribeira da Janela   A 3

Location: 45km north-west of Funchal
Altitude: about 450m
Population: about 800

Location and importance

The village of Ribeira da Janela lies to the south-east of Porto Moniz (see entry) on the river of the same name. The village is located at the point where the river leaves its deeply indented valley and enters the sea. In front of the river mouth three sheer rocks tower up out of the sea, of which one, the Ilhéu da Ribeira da Janela, on account of its natural window-like breach, has given the village its name (Portuguese "janela" = window).

Ribeira da Janela has had an important role in the construction of water-power stations, which began in the 1970s under the Salazar dictatorship. Today there are four such power stations on Madeira, but only a comparatively modest amount of the islanders' electricity needs are met by them. In the next few years it is expected that water-power will be much more extensively used, although a lack of available water could hamper these plans. In addition to water-power, part of the island's electrical energy needs are produced from wind turbines, as for example on the peninsula of Ponta de São Lourenço and the plateau of Paúl da Serra (see entries).

Around Ribeiro Frio are many footpaths which all go through mainly unspoilt scenery ▶

Sights

*Landscape

The village of Ribeira da Janela does not have any important sights. Nevertheless, there is a walk lasting about four hours along the Levada da Central da Ribeira da Janela which is very enjoyable. It begins and ends at the car park above Lamaceiros, a village situated just before Porto Moniz (and the site of a water reservoir which supplies the water-power station), and passes through some exceptionally imposing scenery.

Ribeiro Frio   C 6

Location: 14km north of Funchal
Altitude: 860m
Population: about 500

Location and importance

On the far side of the Poiso Pass the road to Faial takes a winding course downhill through wooded mountain scenery and after 3km reaches Ribeiro Frio (literally "cold stream").

Sights

Trout farming

The only trout farm on Madeira is at Ribeiro Frio. The fish (about 90,000 each year) are reared in terraced ponds which are supplied with oxygen-rich water from the Ribeiro Frio river. The trout are sold to restaurants and other gastronomic firms or put back in streams all over the island, which would otherwise have no fish, so that they can be caught by anglers.

"Victor's Bar" is a restaurant full of atmosphere where freshly-caught trout are served in many different ways or are available to be taken away. They are particularly delicious when freshly smoked and filled with a rasher of bacon.

Parque Florestal

The Parque Florestal, a nature conservation area, begins at the back of "Victor's Bar". Its aim is to protect the island's original lauraceous woodland, which still grows here. There are also many endemic plants here which it is intended to prevent from dying out.

*Walk to the Balções viewpoint

From Ribeiro Frio there is an excellent path which follows the Levada do Furado to the Balções viewpoint. The reward for anyone undertaking the hour-long walk (there and back) is a marvellous view over to the highest points on Madeira: Pico Ruivo, Pico das Torres and Pico do Arieiro.

Assuming an adequate level of fitness and a good foothold, it is possible to walk along the Levada do Furado all the way to Portela. The distance is about 10km and the path passes through some of the most spectacular scenery on Madeira.

Santa Cruz   C 7

Location: 17km north-east of Funchal
Altitude: about 0–150m
Population: about 10,000

Location and importance

The fishing town of Santa Cruz is one of the oldest settlements on the island and lies on the south-east coast of Madeira. Up to now the proximity of Santa Catarina Airport has mercifully restricted tourist development in the town. The little harbour with its shingle beach is now edged by newly planted palm trees; not far away are the "Praia das Palmeiras" bathing facilities. Catching ornamental fish is quite an important element of the local economy.

Sights

The old part of the town presents a remarkably unified picture. In the centre stands the three-aisled Manueline parish church of São Salvador. It was built in 1833 on the remains of an older chapel, from which a gravestone (1470) survives. The sacristy now contains 16th c. azulejos which once adorned the Franciscan convent of "Nossa Senhora da Piedade", which had to be pulled down to make way for the construction of the airport (other tiles from this convent are now on display in the Quinta das Cruzes in Funchal, see entry).

★★ Townscape

The 16th c. town hall is decorated with Manueline stonemasonry. The court building was renovated only a few years ago and ranks as one of the finest on Madeira. Nearby is a remarkable curved flight of steps.

To the west across the harbour bay stands a small fortress dating from 1706, which is privately owned and is therefore not open to public viewing.

It is worth paying a visit to the market hall, where a wide range of fish is available, as well as meat, fruit and vegetables from the surrounding area. The building is decorated with tile paintings from the recent period.

Market hall

On the other side of the airport road EN 101 continues westwards, initially a fast road, using the route of the future motorway to Funchal, and then on the old coast road which passes through a fertile vegetable-growing area. In past times bananas, sugar cane and vines were extensively grown here. More and more, fields which were once cultivated are now lying fallow, as they have more potential profit if they are set aside as land for future building.

Surroundings

Santa Catarina Airport

The road continues past the above-mentioned junction, along by the sea, past the tourist settlement of Agua de Penha to the airport on the Ponta de Santa Catarina.

Location

Known popularly as the "aircraft-carrier", in the 1960s the airport replaced the former landing facilities on the military airbase on Porto Santo, from where visitors had to face a two to three hour boat journey to get across to the main island.

After weather considerations forced plans to build a modern airport on the misty plateau of Paúl da Serra to be abandoned, it was decided to go for the small and comparatively gentle promontory of Ponta de Santa Catarina. The airport, which opened in 1964, possessed a 1600m long runway and could only take smaller aircraft.

In order to open up the island to modern mass tourism, the runway was extended by 1750m into the sea in 1985, using concrete columns. A second extension of 2780m towards Machico is currently under construction. Owing to the great depth of the ocean bed at this point, the runway is going to be skewed round several degrees to the north into the bay and there anchored on new supports at a lesser depth, though still 70–80m.

A model of the planned new airport site stands in the foyer (1st floor) of the airport building.

Santana   B 6

Location: 42km north of Funchal
Altitude: 420m
Population: about 4500

Location and importance

Santana is the main locality in the comarca of Santana, the most fertile area of Madeira. With its thatched houses surrounded by the most prolific array of flowers imaginable, Santana is one of the most picturesque places on the island. Potato, maize and wheat growing are important and Santana is also a centre for Madeiran embroidery.

Sights

★★Townscape

The most striking feature in Santana are the Casas de Colmos – houses with pointed gables whose thatched roofs extend right down to the ground. Nowadays, though, these houses are becoming fewer and fewer in number, so much so that the town council felt impelled to erect two new houses in this style right next to the town hall. There is a thoroughly practical reason for this style of building: the roof gives the interior of the house a large degree of protection from the rigours of the weather. Some residents of the Casas de Colmos are so hospitable that they will invite visitors in to see the inside of their houses.

Festa dos Compadres

Every year in February the Festa dos Compadres takes place in Santana. The theme of the festival is the settling of a marital dispute by assembling a special court. The two parties – husband and wife –

Typical Santana houses with steep roofs down to the ground

are represented by straw dolls, while the "hearing" is not short of allusions to current political topics and village events. After the judgment is given by the court, the straw dolls are burnt. The ensuing festival with music and dancing lasts well into the small hours of the morning.

To the east of Santana rises the tiny mountain of Garajoa, from the top of which there is a good view over the east coast of Madeira. It is reached by taking a turning off road no. 101.

★Garajoa viewpoint

From Santana it is well worth while making a trip to the refuge house Casa das Queimadas (alt. 883m), and then continuing on foot southwards to the Parque das Queimadas on the slopes of Pico Ruivo (1861m), which can also be climbed from here.

★Recommended trip

Santo da Serra   C 7

Location: 22km north-east of Funchal
Altitude: 675m
Population: about 2000

Santo da Serra – its full name is actually Santo António da Serra – lies on a meadowy plateau in the eastern part of Madeira and has always enjoyed the reputation of being a select resort. In the 18th c., in particular, the village was the preferred residence of many of the rich merchant families in Funchal, who had their fashionable quintas built here. Today Santo (António) da Serra is known for its splendidly located golf course.

Location and importance

A beautiful view from Miradouro dos Ingleses to the peninsula of Ponta de São Lourenço

Sights

★Quinta da
Junta

The gardens which originally formed part of the Quinta da Junta (also known as Quinta Santo da Serra) have been turned into a public park. Situated in the centre of the village, it is a popular place with visitors. The park, which once formed part of the Blandy family estate, contains a small animal enclosure with deer and birds of prey.

★Miradouro dos
Ingleses

From the Miradouro dos Ingleses (Englishmen's Viewpoint), a platform hewn from the rock, there is a marvellous view over the imposing landscape. It extends in an easterly direction as far as Machico and the peninsula of Ponta de São Lourenço (see entries). The viewpoint gets its name from English merchants who stationed a look-out post here. Its object was to inform the merchants of Funchal when a merchant ship was due to arrive.

São Jorge   B 6

Location: 49km north of Funchal
Altitude: about 10–150m
Population: about 3000

Location and
importance

The little town of São Jorge lies on the north coast of Madeira. The final section of the road to São Jorge goes along numerous bends and twists and past the "As Cabanhas" viewpoint (with picnic area) before ending right in the centre of the town. The fact that practically all the tourist coaches stop here has contributed to the modest prosperity which the residents of São Jorge enjoy. Fruit and vegetable

A narrow road with many bends runs along the north coast of Madeira

growing are also important and many of the willow canes used in the basketry industry are cut here.

Sights

São Jorge possesses a remarkable Baroque church dating from the 18th c., which was built on the site of an earlier 15th c. building destroyed by flooding in 1660. While the exterior of the present church looks austere and unassuming, the interior is resplendent with lavish gilded wood carvings, beautiful altarpieces and exceptionally ornate azulejos.

★★Igreja do São Jorge

Of interest in the cemetery above the church is the tomb of the American, Miss Turner, who died in 1925. She was well-known for her tearoom, a popular meeting-place for English people living on Madeira.

Cemetery

Not far from the church is the Quinta de São Jorge, which was once lived in by Dr João Francisco de Oliveira. He made a name for himself not just as a scientist and doctor, but also as a diplomat. As the large estate is today still privately owned, it is not possible to visit it.

Quinta de São Jorge

From the nearby Ponta de São Jorge, which juts out into the sea and has a lighthouse, there is a wide view across the north coast as far as Porto Moniz in the west and Porto da Cruz in the east (see entries).

★Ponta de São Jorge

São Vicente   B 4

Location: 54km north of Funchal
Altitude: about 15–350m
Population: about 6000

On the far side of the pass of Boca da Encumeada (see entry) the road goes down through Rosário to the coast at São Vicente. The picturesque little town lies on the left bank of the river of the same name and not far from where it flows into the sea. It is surrounded by wild mountainous scenery and is a good starting-point for the ascent of Pico dos Tarquinhos (1524m) and Pico Ruivo do Paúl (1642m), from both of which there are magnificent views of the mountains. Other worthwhile trips can be made into the Paúl da Serra area. São Vicente was hit by a landslide in 1928 and partially submerged.

Location and importance

Sights

São Vicente offers a very unified looking townscape. This is in no small measure due to the fact that the inhabitants took concerted action to maintain the appearance of their houses and all renovated them in the 1980s. Their reward was not just a conservation prize but also a constant increase in visitors, bringing prosperity to the town.

★Townscape

The beautiful 17th c. Baroque parish church is well worth seeing. The interior is richly fitted out with gilded wood carvings and paintings. Particular attention should be paid to the picture of the patron saint, Vincent of Valencia, on the painted ceiling. On the cobbled square outside the church, the attributes of Saint Vincent are represented (two ravens defending the saint's corpse, and the sailing ship from which according to legend he was thrown into the sea and later washed up on land).

★Igreja do Santo Vicentius

Seixal

Capela São
Roque

Where the Ribeira de São Vicente flows into the Atlantic, next to a
soberly constructed bridge, there is a prominent rock, on top of which
stands a cross which can be seen from some distance. In its shadow
the little Capela São Roque was built in 1692. The pebble mosaics on
the façade are of interest.

Seixal   B 3

Location: 57km north of Funchal
Altitude: about 10–350m
Population: about 900

Location and
importance

About halfway between Porto Moniz and São Vicente (see entries) lies
the little village of Seixal, only a short distance from the coast road
with its wonderful views. The village is situated on the slopes of a
mountain spur, surrounded by vine terraces. It is known less for any
notable sights than for its excellent Sercial wine. The vines used to
produce it are grown only with the utmost toil and difficulty. As a protection from the strong winds which blow off the Atlantic, the vine
plots are surrounded by waist-high hedges.

★★Coast road

Beyond Seixal the most impressive section of the northern coast road
begins and indeed one of the finest stretches of scenery in the whole
of Madeira. The road has had to be elaborately carved out of the rock,
using every available technological device, including tunnels and
bridges, in order to overcome the difficulties posed by the almost vertical cliffs. The road is at times poised above the raging waters of the
ocean in the shadow of mighty mountain walls – hovering, as it were,
between sky and ocean.

★Ribeira do
Inferno

About 2km beyond Seixal there is a viewpoint which affords an awe-
inspiring view of the gorge through which the Ribeira do Inferno enters the sea. Afterwards the road continues for another 6km, partly
through tunnels underneath the rushing water of the river, until it
reaches São Vicente (see entry).

The yacht harbour of Funchal: a port of call for Atlantic ▶
yachtsmen and a departure point for sailing round Madeira

**Practical
Information
from A to Z**

Air Travel

Airport   Santa Catarina, Madeira's airport, is at Santa Cruz about 11 miles east of Funchal. For independent travellers the best way to cover this distance is by taxi from the rank in front of the arrival hall. Visitors on package holidays will find coaches waiting outside the arrival hall.

Flights   Flights are covered in the Getting to Madeira entry (see p.149). All flights to Porto Santo stop at Madeira first.

Airport information   Santa Catarina airport, Madeira: tel. 52 49 41
Porto Santo airport: tel. 98 23 79/98 27 11

Airlines   TAP – Air Portugal
Rua Dr. Antonio J. Almeida, Funchal
tel. 23 92 10, fax 23 92 03
Individual reservations: tel. 23 92 05
Group reservations: tel. 23 92 30
TAP has another office in Funchal on Avenida do Mar, and an office on Porto Santo (tel. 98 22 72).

Angling

Big-game fishing   A number of operators offer whole or half-day fishing trips and charters out of Funchal harbour; to take part in such a trip apply directly to one of them. Several record catches have been recorded in the past, mostly tuna but the mighty blue marlin as well.

Banks

See Money

Bathing Beaches

Madeira   Madeira is not an island of golden sands and bathing beaches. The few beaches it does have are either pebble beaches, such as Ribeira Brava at Santa Cruz, or beaches of black sand, like Prainha and Caniçal on the Ponta de São Lourenço peninsula.
   One alternative, though, when the weather is fine, is to swim in the natural pools created by the lava formations at Caniço and Porto Moniz, but make sure to take bathing shoes with a good grip. A number of Funchal hotels also have these natural-type lidos.

Porto Santo   The island of Porto Santo, unlike Madeira, has golden sands in plenty, and its Campo de Baixo, which stretches for about 5$\frac{1}{2}$ miles, is one of Portugal's longest beaches. Since this is a favourite spot with many Madeiran families at the weekends, the best time to visit is during the week when it is not so crowded.

Swimming   See entry

◄ In the Zona Velho, the restored old town of Funchal, are many open-air restaurants

Begging

The steadily increasing flow of visitors has led to a problem with begging which tourists have in part brought on themselves. The beggars are mostly children, but can be the old, sick and disabled as well, and they usually target the popular tourist spots. It is up to the visitor to decide whether the best way to deal with the problem is to encourage them by giving them money or simply hand out a couple of sweets brought from home.

Business Hours

See Opening Times

Cafés, Bars and Bistros

Calling in somewhere for a small black coffee (bica) is absolutely no problem on Madeira since the locals are very fond of their little café-type bars, and there is one on almost every corner. Here people meet for a chat usually before or after a meal, or simply to while away the time, and the prices are very reasonable. For a more substantial cup of coffee or even a bite to eat it is more usual to go to a hotel or restaurant.

In the centre of Funchal and below the Cathedral the street leading down to the harbour has a couple of cafés with tables outside where light meals and snacks are served as well as tea and coffee. Their central location also makes these good bases from which to explore the northern and eastern parts of the city.

Quite close by, off Rua da Carreira, light meals are also obtainable at O Pátio, the café-restaurant in the patio garden in front of the Vicente Photography Museum. Another particularly pleasant place to take tea or coffee is Pluma, in the garden of a little quinta opposite the Dom Jõao Hotel (13b Rua das Maravilhas).

Outside Funchal every little place has at least one café which is the local meeting point and where the inevitable bica, with or without milk and sugar, is served.

In Funchal

Outside Funchal

Camping

Madeira's only campsite is at Porto Moniz; since the number of plots is limited it pays to book in advance either through the tourist office (see Information) or with the campsite direct (tel. 85 24 47).

Madeira

There is another official campsite on Porto Santo, and bookings can also be made through the tourist office.

Porto Santo

It is possible to camp off-site provided you have obtained permission beforehand from the landowner or the relevant forestry officials, but impromptu camping elsewhere is not a wise move because it can do untold harm to wildlife and the countryside.

Off-site camping

Car Hire

Exploring Madeira in a hire-car is a very pleasant prospect indeed and in Funchal there are plenty of reputable car-hire firms with fleets of well-

Booking

135

maintained vehicles. These can be booked on arrival at Santa Catarina airport or through the larger hotels.

Rates
Car-hire rates on Madeira are relatively cheap and vary according to the season, length of rental, and size of vehicle. The daily rate for a small car (e.g. Renault Twingo) is around 4400 Esc. and for one in the middle of the range about 7000 Esc., plus 12% VAT. Most car-hire firms accept payment by credit card (see Currency) and give discounts for longer rental periods.

Driving licence, insurance
Drivers must be at least 21 years old and be able to produce their driving licence – in some cases they need to have held a licence for at least a year. While third-party insurance is included in the basic price it is advisable to have fully comprehensive insurance as well for the period of the rental.

Convertibles
The thought of driving around Madeira in a convertible with the top down may appear very tempting, but is not something to be recommended. Although the car-hire firms usually have convertibles on their books they sometimes forget to point out that driving on Madeira does have its drawbacks, especially on coastal roads and on entering and leaving tunnels, when anyone travelling in an open-topped car is likely to be drenched by water cascading down from the rocks above.

Car-hire firms (selection)

Atlas
Rua Alegria (Funchal); tel. 22 31 00, fax 74 12 12

Avis
164 Largo António Nobre (Funchal); tel. 76 45 46, fax 76 52 40
Santa Catarina airport; tel. 52 43 92
c/o Hotel Monumental Lido (Funchal); tel. 76 45 46

Budget
c/o Hotel Duas Torres, Estrada Monumental (Funchal); tel. 76 65 18, fax 76 56 19 (Machico branch in Centro Comercial; tel. 96 23 05)

Futuro Rent-a-car
Avenida do Infante (Funchal); tel. 22 07 21/22 06 33, fax 22 22 20 (branch in Centro Comercial Avenida)

Lidorent Rent-a-car
Edificio Alto Lido, Estrada Monumental (Funchal); tel. 76 14 20/ 76 14 21, fax 76 16 35

Casino

See Nightlife

Chemists

The sign for a chemist (farmácia) is a green cross. Chemists are usually open Mon.–Fri. 9am–1pm and 3–7pm, Sat. 9am–1pm. The address of the nearest chemist on duty at night and on Sundays (farmácia de serviço) is displayed in each chemist's shop window. English-speaking visitors can make purchases from Botica Inglesa, Rua Câmara Pestaria 23–25. Funchal. Tel. 22 01 58.

Children

Although Madeira has no theme parks or similar child-centred amusements it does have simpler pleasures which children can enjoy. The fact that the best beach is on the neighbouring island of Porto Santo is more than made up for by the exciting walks they can join in along the levadas for example – grown-ups are not the only ones who like exploring the countryside and discovering the different kinds of wildlife. Madeira's hotels are also usually adapted to catering for families with children, and most of them have swimming pools and special children's holiday programmes.

Clothing

As a rule all that is necessary for a holiday in Madeira is suitable clothing for the climate and the occasion. For walking in the mountains, for example, trousers are more practical than shorts and sensible footwear, but not necessarily walking boots, should be worn. Also take some kind of waterproof to cope with sudden showers.

For evenings in a smart hotel gentlemen are expected to wear a jacket and collar and tie.

Suitable clothing

Since the sunniest skies can suddenly turn to showers make sure to take an umbrella. A rainproof jacket of some sort to cope with a surprise downpour could also prove very useful.

Take an umbrella!

Crime

Crime-rates in Madeira are no higher than elsewhere in Europe but just the same only carry as much cash you are likely to need and always keep an eye on valuables such as cameras. Never leave luggage unattended at airports or on board ship – thieves are always on the lookout even when you are not.

Take the usual precautions

Almost every hotel has a safe where passports, air tickets, etc. as well as cash and travellers' cheques can be left. Take advantage of it, since no hotel anywhere in the world will assume liability for the possible theft of valuables from hotel rooms.

Use the hotel safe

Currency

The Portuguese unit of currency is the escudo (Esc.) which is (theoretically) sub-divided into 100 centavos, and its symbol – the dollar sign $ – is written between the escudos and the centavos. There are banknotes for 500, 1000, 5000 and 10,000 Esc. and coins in denominations of 1, $2^{1}/_{2}$, 5, 10, 20, 50, 100 and 200 Esc. and 50 and 10 centavos.

Currency

Membership of the European Union means there are no restrictions on how much foreign currency a private individual can take into Portugal, although amounts in excess of one million escudos should be declared on entry.

The export of local currency is limited to 10,000 Esc. and of foreign currency to the equivalent of 500,000 Esc. or the amount declared on entry.

Currency import and export

Foreign currency (cash, Eurocheques, travellers' cheques) can be changed or cashed in banks. These are open Mon.–Fri. 8.30–11.45am and 1–2.45pm. Funchal also has a number of automatic money-changing cash dispensers which can be used outside banking hours.

It is worth remembering, though, that as is usually the case with

Changing money

countries that have a weak currency, it pays to change money before going to Portugal and any money changed back at the end of the holiday will probably be at a loss.

Eurocheques | Eurocheques can be cashed up to an amount of 35,000 Esc.; proof of identity is required as well as a Eurocheque card. If this card is lost telephone immediately the relevant number in the country of issue so that it can be cancelled at once.

Credit cards | Madeiran banks, hotels, restaurants, retailers, tour operators, and the duty-free shop at Santa Catarina airport, accept all the major international credit cards (American Express, Bank Americard/Visa, Mastercard/Eurocard, Diners Club).

When buying anything by credit card always check the amounts written on the original slip and the copy to make sure that they tally.

Report the loss of any credit cards immediately so that they can be cancelled.

Customs Regulations

European Single Market | The advent of the single market within the European Union has meant that EU residents visiting Portugal can broadly speaking bring in and take out items for their personal use duty-free. There are, however, still some upper limits on duty-free allowances for incoming items, e.g. 800 cigarettes for travellers aged over 17, 10 litres of spirits and 90 litres of wine. For goods bought in duty-free shops – due to be phased out by the end of 1999 – the same limits apply as for travellers from non-EU countries (see below).

Entry from non-EU countries | Duty-free allowances for travellers from non-EU countries: 200 cigarettes or 50 cigars or 250 g smoking tobacco (travellers aged over 17 only); 2 litres wine; 2 litres sparkling wine or 1 litre spirits over 22% proof or 2 litres liqueurs or fortified wine under 22% proof.

Re-entry to EU countries | The upper limits for duty-free allowances for visitors (aged over 18) returning from Portugal to EU countries such as Britain and Ireland are: 800 cigarettes and 400 cigarillos and 200 cigars and 1 kg tobacco, 10 litres spirits over 22% proof and 20 litres below 22% proof and 90 litres of wine, plus an unlimited amount of perfume and toilet water.

Re-entry to non-EU countries | For countries outside the European Union the allowances are as follows: Australia 250 cigarettes or 50 cigars or 250 g tobacco, 1 litre spirits or 1 litre wine; Canada 200 cigarettes and 50 cigars and 1 kg tobacco, 1.14 litres spirits or wine; New Zealand 200 cigarettes or 50 cigars or 250 g tobacco, 1.125 litres spirits and 4.5 litres wine; South Africa 400 cigarettes and 50 cigars and 250 g tobacco, 1 litre spirits and 2 litres wine; USA 200 cigarettes or 100 cigars or 2 kg of tobacco or proportionate amounts of each, 1 litre spirits or 1 litre wine.

Diplomatic Representation

Consulates in Funchal

United Kingdom | Avenida Zarco 2; tel. 22 12 21
(Commonwealth citizens as well)

United States of America | Avenida Luós de Camões, Ed. Infante,
Block B, 4th floor; tel. 74 34 29

Embassies in Lisbon

Avenida da Liberdade 244; tel. (01) 52 33 50	**Australia**
Avenida da Liberdade 144-156; tel. (01) 347 48 92	**Canada**
Rua da Imprensa a Estrela 1; tel. (01) 396 15 69	**Eire**
Avenida Luís Bivar 10/10a; tel. (01) 53 50 41	**South Africa**
Rua S. Domingos à Lapa 37; tel. (01) 396 11 91	**United Kingdom**
Avenida das Forças Armadas 16; tel. (01) 726 66 00	**United States of America**

Drinking Water

The drinking water provided in Madeira's hotels and restaurants comes from the Portuguese mainland. It is of a high standard and even travellers with sensitive stomachs will find they can drink it with impunity.

Electricity

The electricity supply is 220 AC, with continental two-pin plugs. Most standard European plugs can be used in the big hotels, but American flat-pin plugs require a transformer and an adaptor.

Emergency Services

General emergency number (police, fire, ambulance): 115

Outpatient/Casualty Department
Centro Médico da Sé, 42 Rua dos Murcas:
tel. 23 01 27/23 17 79-82

Clínica de Santa Catarina, 115 Rua 5 de Outubro
(24-hr. casualty):
tel. 74 11 27

Medical emergency service
Clínica de Santa Luzia, 5 Rua da Torrinha
(24-hr. casualty):
tel. 23 34 34

The police on Madeira are very helpful and can be found everywhere

Dental emergency service
Clínica Dentária Cinco de Outubro, 79a Rua 5 de Outubro:
tel. 22 82 17

Poisons emergency line
Emergências Médicas: tel. 795 01 43

Environmental Awareness

See Green Tourism

Events Calendar

What's On	Listings in English of what's on can be found in the *Madeira Island Bulletin*, the monthly free newspaper obtainable from the local tourist offices.
February/March	As in nearly all Catholic countries Carnival plays an important part in Madeiran life. The highpoint of the four days of festivities is a colourful weekend procession ending in general jollification on Funchal's town hall square. There is another procession on Shrove Tuesday which is for the general public rather than organised groups. Each place on the island also has its own Carnival celebrations.
April	The colourful flower festival at the end of April is one of the most important events in Madeira's calendar. Although it lasts for several days the one event not to be missed is the parade of floral floats through the streets of Funchal in which groups from all over the island take part.
May/June	The Musical Weekends of Madeira and the Madeira Music Festival, held mostly in Funchal in May and June, bring together orchestras and famous international classical music performers. The concert venues include Funchal's theatre and churches.
July	Like the rest of Portugal every little place in Madeira has its own patron saint and holds annual festivals in their honour. These take place at weekends from July through to September, and culminate in a pilgrimage, or "romaria", on the Sunday when everyone processes through the streets behind the saint's image. Throughout the festival there are stalls selling Madeiran specialities. Contact the Funchal tourist office to find out when and where these local festivals take place (see also Festivals and Holidays).
August	The Madeira Wine Rally has been an annual event on the first weekend in August since 1959. It covers the whole island and points won in this gruelling cross-country event count towards the Europa Cup.
September	The Madeira Wine Festival marks the start of the grape harvest in mid-September. It is celebrated in a number of villages, but is probably at its most impressive in Estreito Câmara de Lobos. Funchal, too, puts on special events with Madeiran folklore and wine-tastings.
December	Christmas and New Year: Funchal is lit up for Christmas from December 8th; midnight mass in Funchal Cathedral is one of the season's highlights, but Madeira's most spectacular festival is New Year's Eve, when visitors from all over the world flock to see in the new year to the accompaniment of a mammoth display of fireworks.
Holidays	See Festivals and Holidays

Excursions

Island tours	Funchal has a number of tour operators who specialise in whole- or half-day coach tours of the island. These are accompanied by multilingual guides, and for a first-time visit to Madeira it is well worth making a tour

of this kind to get a general impression of the island. Coaches pick up and drop at all the main hotels. Names and addresses of the various companies can be found in Madeira's *Yellow Pages*.

Madeira, with its clear blue waters, is one of Europe's best places for scuba-diving and viewing marine life. To explore this fantastic underwater world without getting wet feet try the "Carol", a glass-bottomed boat built in 1994. For information contact:
Madeirasub, Actividades Marítimas Turisticas; tel. 22 94 33

Glass-bottomed boat

See Walking

Levada walks

See entry

Car Hire

For half-day trips and 2¹/₂ hour sunset sails on the yacht "Albatroz" with up to 20 passengers contact:
Albatroz Organization, Funchal Marina; tel. 22 03 27

Sailing trips

Festivals and Holidays

The Madeirans love their high days and holidays and there are festivals throughout the whole year, so the visitor would have to be really unlucky not to be able to join in at least one while on the island.
   Many are religious festivals in the form of romárias, pilgrimages in honour of the local patron saint. The most spectacular is the Feast of the Assumption in Monte, just above Funchal, on August 15th when pilgrims from all over the island flock to the festival of Our Lady of

Madeira is a great place for festivals

As well as official holidays there are many spontaneous festivities – here University students celebrate passing their examinations

Monte. The highpoint here is the promessa, when pilgrims make their way up the steps of the church of Nossa Senhora do Monte on their knees to fulfil promises made when times were hard.

Everywhere in Madeira has its own romária when the local people processes through the streets and the whole place is given over to music, dancing and of course specially grilled food. The most picturesque romárias are in Ribeira Brava (on June 29th, Feast of St Peter), Machico (last Sunday in August), and Caniçal (third Sunday in September, including a seaborne procession of fishing boats).

Madeira also celebrates Carnival when the highpoint is the weekend parade through Funchal and the streets fill with dancing to the Brazilian beat of the samba. April is marked by the Flower Festival and yet another colourful parade through Funchal, this time of floral floats.

June sees the Madeira Music Festival with concerts by internationally renowned singers and musicians. The village of Estreito de Câmara de Lobos is worth a visit in September for the grand festival that marks the start of the grape harvest.

The run-up to Christmas begins officially on December 8th when Funchal's Christmas lights are switched on and continues with musical and folklore events culminating in the celebration of midnight mass on Christmas Eve in Funchal Cathedral. The highpoint of the year, though, comes on New Year's Eve with a spectacular firework display enjoyed not just by all the locals but by the passengers on many cruise ships moored offshore and in the harbour for this very special occasion.

Public holidays	Besides the official national and seasonal public holidays listed below Madeira has a number of local holidays such as August 21st, when there is a public holiday in Funchal while the rest of the island carries on as normal. The dates of many of the traditional and religious festivals and holidays also vary from place to place. Ask at the local tourist office (see Information) for details.
National	January 1st (New Year); April 25th (Liberation Day commemorating the Carnation Revolution on April 25th 1974); May 1st (Labour Day); June 10th (Portugal Day on the anniversary of the death of Luís de Camões); July 1st (discovery of Madeira); August 15th (Assumption); October 5th (Republic Day); November 1st (All Saints Day); December 1st (Restoration Day commemorating the restoration of Portugal's independence from Spain); December 8th (Feast of Immaculate Conception); December 25th (Christmas Day); December 26th (Feast of St Stephen)
Seasonal	Shrove Tuesday (Carnival, February/March); Ash Wednesday (February/March); Palm Sunday (May/June); Good Friday (May/June); Corpus Christi (June)

Food and Drink

Madeiran fare	The ethnic diversity of the Madeirans is reflected in their bill of fare although obviously this is mainly typically Portuguese cuisine which tends to be wholesome and hearty but not terribly adventurous. Given that Portugal is still one of Europe's relatively poor countries the choice of dishes on the restaurant menu can be rather limited, except of course where tourists are specifically catered for. If there is one underlying principle to Portuguese food, though, it is to make the most of the fresh local produce available, adding flavour with herbs such as thyme, rosemary, and bay leaves, plus liberal amounts of olive oil.
Basic meals	As in other southern countries breakfast is quite a spartan affair and only the big tourist hotels provide cheese, cold meats and eggs in addition to

the basic coffee, bread, butter and jam. More thought is given to midday and evening meals which usually consist of two or even three courses.

Fresh bread is served with every meal. The traditional Paõ de Casa, with a touch of sweet potato, is particularly tasty.

Madeira's own special soup is Sopa de tomate e cebola, made from tomatoes and onions topped at the last minute with a poached egg. Another favourite is the famous Caldo verde made from shredded cabbage either as a clear soup or thickened to a creamy broth (connoisseurs of Portuguese cuisine swear by the latter albeit distinctly calorific method of preparation).

Local specialities
Soups

CALDEIRADA À LA REID'S

Fish caught off Madeira's coasts forms the basis of a typically Madeiran soup as prepared by the head chef at Reid's Hotel.

Ingredients:

*250 gr. red mullet, 300 gr. monkfish, 300 gr. sea bream
300 gr. grey mullet, 4 tomatoes, 1 carrot,
1 courgette, 1 medium-sized onion, 1 small leek,
2 cloves of garlic, 1 medium head of celery, 2 bayleaves,
1 sprig of thyme, 10 gr. ground caraway seeds, 5 cl. olive oil,
20 gr. butter, salt, freshly ground pepper, 2 cl. white wine*

Preparation:

*Scale, fillet and chop the fish into medium-sized pieces
Skin and cut up the tomatoes, finely chop the onion and garlic
Peel and clean other vegetables, cut them into fine strips
Boil up the fish-bones, etc. to make a fish stock
Gently heat up the olive oil in a casserole, add onion, garlic
and tomatoes, dilute with white wine and allow to boil briefly
Add fish stock and simmer for 35 minutes
Add chopped fish and remaining vegetables, season and
simmer gently for 5 minutes. Then serve up in the casserole.*

Although pork and beef seldom grace the tables of the local people they are of course on the menu of every restaurant. The local meat speciality is Espetada da Madeira, beef kebab traditionally skewered on a laurel twig and then grilled over an open fire. Also served are various kinds of escalopes and steaks, including typically Portuguese beef steak in the form of Bife à portuguesa.

For special occasions the local favourite is roast suckling pig (Leitão assado) or roast kid (Cabrito).

Meat dishes

While chicken (Frango) is popular and a relatively cheap item on every menu, turkey, duck and game-birds seldom feature.

Poultry

Madeira naturally has an abundance of fish dishes but other sea creatures such as lobster, crayfish, crab, octopus and small shellfish are always fresh and usually quite cheap too. A glance at the fish tanks in many of the restaurants gives an idea of the diversity of Madeira's underwater life.

Fish and seafood

143

Have some Madeira m'dear –
the older the better!

The wine for which Madeira is famous undergoes a stranger process here than any other wine in the world. And anyone who knows about such things would shake their head in disbelief unless they had savoured the exceptional qualities of Sercial, Verdelho and Malmsey. But how this all came about was really down to chance . . .

To start at the beginning, when the island's first settlers cleared the land by burning down many of the trees they soon found that the wood ash had rendered the already rich volcanic soil even more fertile. But before long they realised that the wine from the imported vines grown in this soil had a slightly acid tang which took some getting used to. Where chance took a hand was the way they found out that this wine could be given a flavour that would earn it fame world-wide. What happened was that the seafarers who called in at Madeira to stock up with wine before setting out on their voyages of discovery reported an amazing taste transformation after the wine casks had been exposed to the heat of the Tropics. And when they started topping it up with brandy to stop it fermenting Madeira then acquired its distinctive flavour.

The old wine cellar of the Madeira Wine Company in Funchal

The basic process of making wine on Madeira is essentially the same today as it was over four centuries ago, only nowadays it is no longer

Madeira production was very nearly wiped out by the dreaded phylloxera. Many of the vintners had to close down or merge with others, but the

The old sales book is proof that Madeira wine was – and is – exported all over the world

sent on round-the-world voyages but heated up in special lodges called estufas where it is kept for four or five months at a temperature of about 50°C/122°F. Before the wine reaches full maturity it undergoes the solera process, whereby the new wine is put into various quality categories and goes into the criadera, or crêche. From here the casks are stacked in rows (soleras), with each solera holding wine of the same category. In the course of this process new wine is added to old and when it reaches the end of the row the blended wine is tapped and re-casked. Only when it has been kept for a further period, which can last for decades, is the wine finally bottled and ready for drinking.

The history of Madeira's wine has not been without its disasters. In 1850 the vines were hit by the very worst kind of mildew and 20 years later

day was saved by importing hybrid vines from America, which is why nowadays the classic vine types are very few and far between. The year of the wine is equally hard to find on Madeira bottles. This is because as a rule the labels only show the age of the wine – usually between 10 and 15 years old. The notable exception is "vintage" Madeira, made from a single type of grape in a single year and which has been aged for at least 20 years, all of which needless to say is reflected in the price.

What the label will tell you, on the other hand, is the wine type – Sercial, Verdelho, Bual or Malmsey – ranging from dry to very rich and full-bodied. Unlike other wines, though, the degree of sweetness is determined not by the type of grape but by the amount of brandy the wine has been fortified with and the point at which

Food and Drink

Have some Madeira m'dear – the older the better – continued

that brandy has been added. Sercial is the driest and its grapes are not picked until November, while Malmsey, which is an out and out dessert wine, is the richest and sweetest. There are a few other kinds of grape which go to make the humbler Madeiras used by chefs throughout the world for the famous "Sauce Madère".

Madeira has virtually unlimited keeping properties and the wine in bottles that have been opened after a hundred years or more has still been astonishingly fresh and full-bodied.

And how should you store your Madeira? Unlike other wine, which is best stored on its side, Madeira should be kept upright. This is because it no longer needs to absorb oxygen through the cork. Once uncorked, though, it should not be left for too long, something which no connoisseur of such a fine wine should find too difficult...

Madeira's own fish speciality is the Espada which, with its off-putting goggle eyes, may not look attractive but actually tastes delicious. Some restaurants still serve it with the traditional accompaniment of grilled banana.

Another speciality is swordfish (Espadarte) which, like tuna (Atum), sea bream (Pargo) and red mullet (Salmonete), also features on almost every menu. And finally there is Portugal's national dish of salt cod (Bacalhau a Gomes de Sá), usually prepared with onions, garlic, olives and potatoes. Seafood risotto (Arroz de mariscos) is another delicious combination that is worth trying.

Vegetables

White haricot beans braised with bacon and served with a tomato sauce (Feijâo guisado) are firm favourites with the Portuguese and often substantial enough to be a meal in themselves. Green beans are also flavoured with bacon but with the addition of chopped onion and a smattering of garlic.

The main course is usually accompanied by potatoes, French fries or occasionally pasta. Chickpeas (Grâo com tomates) pureed with tomatoes, oil and garlic make another very tasty side dish.

Fruit

A wide choice of exotic fruit is grown on the island. One that stands out as particularly delicious is the custard apple (Anonas or Cherimoya), harvested early in the year and shaped like an irregular golf ball. Buy them when they are semi-ripe and keep them for a few days until they acquire the pale purple patina that shows they have fully ripened. Madeira's mangos (Manga) are quite small, yellow and fibrous but full of flavour.

The insides of the long cones of the Swiss cheese plant, which grows wild and in parks and gardens, have a delicate sweet taste when they are really ripe – hence its Latin name, monstera deliciosa.

The passion flower (Maracujá) both gives off an intoxicating fragrance and has edible fruit.

Confectionery

No-one with a sweet tooth will go short on Madeira. A particular speciality is Bolo de mel, a long-lasting honey-cake that also makes a good souvenir. There is a wide choice of other delicious sweet cakes as well.

Wine is still the traditional drink at mealtimes, and most of the wine drunk at table in Madeira is imported from the Portuguese mainland. The best-known table wine is Vinho verde. Its name, green wine, refers not to colour but the method of production: the grapes are harvested early and only fermented for a short time to give a light acidic wine which then is further fermented in the bottle, thus producing a crisp, often slightly sparkling wine.

Drink
Wine

The wine that for centuries has made Madeira famous the world over is not drunk with food but before or after meals as an aperitif or digestif. Humbler versions also find their way into the kitchen where they are particularly in demand in the preparation of fine sauces.

Madeira wine

There are four types of Madeira. These are named after the main grape used and are of varying degrees of sweetness:

Malmsey   the sweetest and probably also the best of the Madeira wines. It is distinguished by its rich brown colour, has a slight sharpness and is particularly suited for rounding off a good meal.

Bual   is relatively light and not quite as sweet as Malmsey but also makes a good dessert wine.

Verdelho   ranks more as medium dry, with a hint of smoke and honey, and is drunk as an aperitif and a dessert wine.

Sercial   is made from grapes that grow at higher altitudes and are the last to be picked. It has a nutty, dry flavour and makes a good aperitif.

Mineral water (Agua mineral) either still (sem gás) or carbonated (com gás) is readily available, although both tend to be rather flat. The neighbouring island of Porto Santo produces a particularly good mineral water which is supposed to have health-giving properties.

Mineral water

Madeira has all the usual globally marketed soft drinks (Coca Cola, Pepsi Cola, Sprite, etc.) plus the less calorific alternatives of freshly pressed fruit juice.

Soft drinks, coffee

Strong, black coffee (Café or Bica) is inevitably served at the end of a good meal; you can also get Italian-type espresso and cappuccino.

Besides imported beers Madeira also has two beers (Cerveja) brewed on the Portuguese mainland, "Coral", which is more of a lager, and the somewhat stronger "Superbock".

Beer

A typical strong drink on Madeira is Poncha, made from the juice of a lemon, two spoonfuls of honey, 2 cl white rum and 2 cl Aguardente and whisked together in a glass. It is said that Annabelle in Camacha's O Arsénio bar mixes the best Ponchas on the island. The fiery spirit which is the base of this drink is Aguardente, distilled from sugar cane at Porto da Cruz (visits can be made to the distillery). After a heavy meal a glass of Aguardents is a good digestif.

Spirits

In the handling of the wooden whisk lies the secret of a good Poncha

Madeiran Menu

Portuguese	English
pequeno almoço	breakfast
almoço	lunch
jantar	dinner
ceia	late-night snack
antepastos	starters
sopa	soup
sobremesas	dessert
carta (or lista, ementa)	menu
prato do dia	dish of the day
talher	cutlery
colher	spoon
garfo	fork
faca	knife
colher de chá	teaspoon
chávena	cup
prato	plate
copo	glass
guardanapo	serviette

	Portuguese	English
Cooking terms	cozido	boiled
	assado	roast, grilled
Seasonings and ingredients	alho	garlic
	azeitonas	olives
	azeite	olive oil
	cebolas	onions
	mostarda	mustard
	óleo	oil
	pepinos	gherkins
	pimento	peppers
	pimenta	pepper
	sal	salt
	vinagre	vinegar
	vinho	wine
Meat and other dishes	açorda	bread soup
	aves	poultry
	bife	steak
	bife à portuguesa	Portuguese beef
	cabrito assado	roast kid
	caldo verde	Portuguese cabbage soup
	canja	chicken soup with rice
	carneiro	mutton
	churrasco	meat grilled over charcoal
	coelho	rabbit
	corço	lamb
	costeleta de porco	pork chop
	frango	chicken
	frango assado	spit-roast chicken
	javali	wild boar
	lebre	hare
	leitão assado	roast suckling pig
	pata	duck
	peixe	fish
	perdiz	partridge
	perua	turkey

porco	pork	
porco assado	roast pork	
sopa do dia	soup of the day	
sopa de legumes	vegetable soup	
sopa de peixe	fish soup	
sopa de tomate e cebola	tomato and onion soup	
vaca	beef	
vitela	veal	
arroz	rice	Side dishes
batatas	potatoes	
batatas fritas	fried potatoes	
massa(s)	pasta	
pão	bread	
pãozinho	roll	
legumes (hortaliça)	vegetables	Vegetables
couve	cabbage	
couve-flor	cauliflower	
cenouras	carrots	
ervilhas	peas	
espargos	asparagus	
espinafre	spinach	
feijões	beans	
tomates	tomatoes	
salada mista	mixed salad	
arroz doce	rice pudding	Desserts
bolo do mel	honey cake	
compota de maçã	apple compote	
gelado misto	mixed ices	
pêra Helena	poire Hélène	
pudim flan	crême caramel	
sorvete	sorbet	
tarta de amêndoa	almond tart	

Getting to Madeira

Very few airlines have direct flights to Funchal since most scheduled services go via Lisbon. There are, however, regular charter flights to Madeira from Britain and the rest of Europe. Flights from London to Madeira take about 3½ hours.

By air

Madeira is a popular stop on cruise liner itineraries throughout the year, although most spend only one or two days in Funchal harbour.

By sea

Green Tourism

It goes without saying that every self-respecting traveller will want to help protect Madeira's natural beauty. Some hotels even promote environmental awareness by such measures as urging their guests to avoid leaving any unnecessary rubbish – every single item has to be removed from the island and disposed of elsewhere.

Helping to protect Madeira's natural beauty

The following suggestions are just a few ways in which by setting an example you can help to protect Madeira's environment:
1. Do not buy any souvenirs made from plants or animals that are threatened with extinction. If they are on the CITES list of endangered

species (corals, ivory, snakeskin, etc.) they will be confiscated by Customs on your return home in any case.

2. When out walking – especially on the levada trails – keep to the prescribed paths. Besides helping with countryside conservation you will also avoid running into any kind of trouble that could arise from venturing without a guide into parts of Madeira's rough and rocky terrain.

3. Don't leave litter – take your used batteries, film canisters, plastic bags, etc. back to your hotel where they can be disposed of properly.

4. Save on water whenever you can, thus reducing the high energy cost of water treatment, and use eco-friendly detergents so as not to overload the drainage system with chemicals.

5. The underwater flora and fauna are particularly sensitive, so bear this in mind when snorkelling, scuba-diving and boating.

Help for the Disabled

The local tourist offices will be glad to help disabled visitors plan their stay on the island but the options are quite limited. Although taxi-drivers are usually very helpful, the basic obstacle for people with disabilities is the fact that Funchal, like the rest of the island, is extremely hilly, and it is virtually impossible for someone in a wheelchair to negotiate the steep lanes on their own.

Only a few hotels cater for the needs of guests with disabilities (specially adapted rooms, etc.). In some cases access is so steep that wheelchairs cannot get up to the entrance, so check out the situation in advance with the travel agent before booking. Further information for disabled UK visitors is available from: RADAR, 12 City Forum, 250 City Road, London EC1V 8AF; tel. (0171) 250 32 22.

Hotels

Most hotels are in Funchal

Madeira offers a wide choice of accommodation. Hotel beds total around 17,000 in its 118 hotels, of which a good 40% are in the higher category. This, needless to say, is also reflected in the average room rate.

Most hotels are in and around Funchal, where the planned expansion in visitor capacity has mainly centred on the hotel zone west of the city centre, which also has a relatively advanced tourist infrastructure. Generally speaking the cheapest way to holiday in Madeira is on a package deal. Independent travellers will find that they have to pay more for a room than if they go through one of the large tour operators.

Hotel guide

The Portuguese tourist offices (see Information) can supply a comprehensive hotel guide, listing all the necessary information such as room rates, addresses, telephone and fax numbers, etc.

Quintas

Quintas are a Madeiran speciality in Funchal and elsewhere on the island – beautiful old mansions, mostly with lovely gardens, containing country-house type hotels with a limited number of rooms but of a high standard and with more of a personal touch than the big hotels. Details of these are also available from Portuguese tourist offices.

Self-catering

Funchal has plenty of hotels and guest-houses with kitchenettes equipped with everything needed for self-catering and usually with shops close by, either in town or in the hotel.

Reservations

During the summer holidays Madeira is a popular destination with the Portuguese as well as other European holidaymakers, so if possible try to go before or after the peak holiday season.

Funchal is equally crowded around Christmas and New Year, so early reservation is essential for that period.

The following room rates can vary considerably according to the season.   Rates

Category A   over 25,000 Esc,
Category B   10,000–25,000 Esc.
Category C   5000–10,000 Esc.

Hotels in Funchal (selection)

*Carlton Palms Aparthotel, 17 Rua Gorgulho; tel. 76 61 00, fax 76 62 47, 75   Category A
studio apartments. At the heart of this striking modern seafront hotel, just over a mile from the town centre, is a carefully restored 19th c. quinta. Families with children are particularly welcome and children have their own club.

*Carlton Village Hotel, Largo António Nobre; tel. 23 10 31, fax 2 33 77. First opened in 1996, this hotel complex belongs to the Madeira Carlton Hotel (see below) and residents can use the facilities there at no extra charge. The buildings, with 164 accommodation units, are in the traditional style found in the Madeiran countryside. Magnificent gardens.

Casino Park Hotel, Avenida do Infante; tel. 23 31 11, fax 23 31 53, 373 rooms. Although it may not look very impressive seen from the road the Casino Park ranks as one of Madeira's top hotels. Its airy foyer is the height of modern interior design, and most of the rooms have a sea view; comprehensive range of sports and entertainment facilities.

*Cliff Bay Hotel Inter-Continental, Estrada Monumental; tel. 70 70 707, fax 76 25 25, 201 rooms. Part of the Inter-Continental chain, this modern resort hotel only a few minutes' walk from the centre of Funchal caters for its international guests with ultra-comfortable rooms and every kind of facility.

*Madeira Carlton Hotel, Largo António Nobre; tel. 23 10 31, fax 22 27, 375 rooms. A five-star hotel not far from the centre, with a swimming pool, lido, several restaurants and many other facilities plus rooms with superb sea views.

Madeira Palácio, 256 Estrada Monumental; tel. 76 44 76, fax 76 44 77, 253 rooms. Luxury hotel between the centre of Funchal and the hotel zone, with swimming pool, restaurant, coffee shop and hotel shopping.

*Quinta da Bela Vista, 4 Caminho Avista Navios; tel. 76 41 44, fax 76 50 90, 67 rooms. Surrounded by magnificent gardens, the rooms of this 19th c. quinta may lack air-conditioning but are stylishly furnished in keeping with their period.

*Reid's Hotel, 139 Estrada Monumental; tel. 76 30 01, fax 76 44 99, 169 rooms. The legendary Reid's has been Madeira's top hotel for over a century (see Baedeker Special, pp.84–85).

Savoy Hotel, Avenida do Infante; tel. 22 20 31, fax 22 31 03, 361 rooms. Like Reid's the emphasis at the Savoy is on expensive opulence; tastefully furnished rooms, nightclub, large pool, and gardens leading down to its own lido.

Atlantic Palms Hotel, Praia Formosa-Arieiro; tel. 7 00 10 00, fax 76 16 94,   Category B
200 rooms. Superb view of the Atlantic from the balconies of the well-

equipped rooms in this modern hotel which opened in 1995; swimming pool.

Baia Azul Hotel, Estrada Monumental; tel. 76 62 60, fax 76 42 45, 215 rooms. Not far from the centre of town but even closer to the seafront Club Naval lido, this hotel has spacious and comfortable rooms; the best (and quietest) are facing the sea.

Eden Mar Aparthotel, Rua do Gorgulho; tel. 76 22 21, fax 76 19 66, 146 apartments. Located in the centre of the Hotel Zone, the Eden Mar is set in fine gardens and includes squash among its many facilities.

Quinta do Sol, 6 Rua Dr. Pita; tel. 76 41 51, fax 76 62 87, 151 rooms. Not a quinta but a modern hotel, its rather plain concrete façade belies the high degree of comfort afforded by the tastefully furnished rooms within. No sea view, though, from rooms in the newest part of the hotel.

Category C

Mimosa Hotel, Buganvilia Hotel, Estrelicia Hotel, Rue Velha Ajuda; tel. Mimosa, 76 50 21; Buganvilia, 76 50 15; Estrelicia, 76 51 31: fax 76 10 44. Three hotels joined together, but each with its own swimming pool, snackbar, restaurants and nightclub. The rooms are functional but well-equipped and some have kitchenettes. The steep drive up to the Buganvilia, though, makes disabled access difficult.

Hotels outside Funchal (selection)

Caniço de Baixo

Hotel Dom Pedro Garajau, Sítio Quinta Garajau; tel. 93 44 21, fax 93 24 54, 282 rooms. Category C. Located just under 2 miles from the centre of Caniço, overlooking a cove, this hotel has a kitchenette in each of its functionally furnished rooms. It has an indoor pool for wet weather days.

*Quinta Splendida, Sítio da Vargem; tel. 93 40 27, fax 93 46 88, 85 rooms. Category A. Certainly one of Madeira's loveliest hotels, the Splendida is in the enchanting setting of a large park with groves of sub-tropical trees. It centres on the actual quinta, a carefully restored mansion which boasts a widely acclaimed restaurant as well the loveliest of rooms. The hotel's other rooms are also equipped with every comfort and there is a magnificent view of the Atlantic from the swimming pool.

Hotel Galomar, Caniço de Baixo; tel. 93 44 10, fax 93 45 55, 45 rooms. Category B. On Madeira's southern coast, a few miles from Caniço; most of the well-equipped rooms have a sea-view and a balcony. It has a sauna as well as a squash court and a diving school.

*Hotel Ondamar, Caniço de Baixo; tel. 93 45 66, fax 93 45 55, 51 rooms. Category B. Only $8^{1}/_{2}$ miles from Funchal, this modern hotel is under the same management as the Hotel Galomar where guests can also go sea-bathing or use the swimming pool. The Ondamar has 53 double rooms and 42 studios with kitchenettes.

Machico

Hotel Dom Pedro Baia, Estrada de S. Roque; tel. 96 57 51, fax 96 68 89, 218 rooms. Category C. This Machico hotel is particularly suitable for families with children. The rooms have recently been refurbished and made very comfortable. Sports facilities include tennis, table tennis, darts, volleyball and scuba-diving. There are buses into Funchal.

Prazeres

Hotel Jardim Atlantico; tel. 82 22 00, fax 82 25 22, 97 rooms. Category B. This is particularly suited for walkers and any other visitors in search of peace and quiet away from the hurly burly of Funchal. It has three different room categories but there is very little to choose between them in terms of comfort. The nearest place is Prazeres but for a swim in the sea the hotel also provides transport to the fishing village of Paúl do Mar about 9 miles away.

*Quinta do Furão, Achada do Gramacho; tel. 57 21 32, fax 57 21 31, 42 rooms. Category B. Before it opened as a hotel in 1997 this quinta in Santana on the Gramacho plateau was already well-known as having one of the best restaurants on the island. It is surrounded by vineyards and well-tended gardens, has a swimming pool, and the rooms have every comfort.

Santana

Hotels on Porto Santo (selection)

Residençia Central, 1 Rua Colonel Abel Magno Vasconcelos; tel. 98 22 26, 12 rooms. Category C. The rooms are quite modest but the hotel is in a central location both for the town and the beach, and has a superb view over the sea and the sands.

Vila Baleira

*Hotel Luamar, Cabeço Ponta; tel. 98 41 03, fax 98 31 00, 113 rooms. Category B. A modern, well-managed medium-class hotel on the loveliest part of Porto Santo beach; comfortable rooms, swimming pool and plenty of sports facilities. Free bus several times a day to Vila Baleira.

Information

Portuguese National Tourist Offices abroad:

Abroad

Suite 1005, 60 Bloor Street West
Toronto, Ontario M4W 3B8
Tel. (416) 921 73 76, Fax. (416) 921 13 53

Canada

ICEP 54, Dawson Street
Dublin 2
Tel. 670 91 33

Ireland

22/25a Sackville Street
London W1X 1LY
Tel. (0171) 494 14 41, Fax. 0171 494 1868

United Kingdom

4th Floor, 590 Fifth Avenue
New York NY 10036
Tel. (212) 354 44 03, Fax. (212) 764 61 37

United States

Direcção Regional do Turismo – Região Autónoma da Madeira
16 Avenida M. Arriage, 9000 Funchal
tel. 22 90 56/22 56 58, fax 23 21 51
Open: Mon.–Fri. 9am–8pm, Sat. 9am–6pm

On Madeira

Santa Catarina Airport (arrivals hall); tel. 52 49 33
Open: to coincide with flight arrivals

Machico (in Forte do Amparo); tel. 96 22 89
Open: Mon.–Fri. 9–12 and 2–5pm

Ribeira Brava (in Forte de São Bento); tel. 95 16 75
Open: Mon.–Fri. 9–12 and 2–5pm

Secretaria Regional do Turismo, Cultura e Emigração (in Vila Baleira); tel. 98 23 61

On Porto Santo

Open: Mon.–Fri. 9–12 and 2–5pm
There is also a tourist information office at Porto Santo airport.
Information for visitors arriving by sea is available from the Direcção
Regional do Porto Santo at the harbour or on Rua de João Gonçalves
Zarco (tel. 98 35 65).

Insurance

Holiday insurance

Visitors are strongly advised to ensure that they have adequate holiday insurance, including loss or damage to luggage, loss of currency and jewellery.

Health care

British citizens, like nationals of other European Union countries, are entitled to obtain medical care when on holiday in Portugal. Treatment can be obtained free of charge, but medicines must be paid for. Before leaving home travellers should obtain form E111 which certifies their entitlement to insurance cover and must be presented when seeking reimbursement.

It is essential for visitors from non-EU countries, and advisable for EU nationals, to take out some form of short-term health insurance providing complete cover and possibly avoiding delays. Nationals of non-EU countries should certainly have insurance cover.

See also Crime, Motoring, Travel Documents

Language

Portuguese pronunciation

In spoken Portuguese, the language of Madeira, the stress is normally on the penultimate syllable of a word ending in a vowel or in "m" or "s" and on the last syllable of a word ending in any other consonant. The letters "s" and "z" are both pronounced "sh" at the end of a word, and "c" is pronounced as "k" before a, o and u, and "s" before e and i. Otherwise, as in most Romance languages, letters are largely pronounced in the same way as English, but the words of a sentence are run together much more.

Knowledge of foreign languages

Although the foreign languages Madeirans are most likely to understand include English, you will find it very handy to have at least a smattering of Portuguese.

Cardinal numbers

0	zero	18	dezoito
1	um, uma	19	dezanove
2	dois, duas	20	vinte
3	três	21	vinte-e-um (uma)
4	quatro	22	vinte-e-dois (duas)
5	cinco	30	trinta
6	seis	31	trinta-e-um (uma)
7	sete	40	quarenta
8	oito	50	cinquenta
9	nove	60	sessenta
10	dez	70	setenta
11	onze	80	oitenta
12	doze	90	noventa
13	treze	100	cem, cento
14	catorze	101	cento-e-um (uma)
15	quinze	200	duzentos, -as
16	dezasseis	300	trezentos, -as
17	dezassete	400	quatrocentos, -as

500	quinhentos, -as	900	novecentos, -as
600	seiscentos, -as	1000	mil
700	setecentos, -as	2000	dois (duas) mil
800	oitocentos, -as	1 million	um milhão de

1st	primeiro, -a	11th	undécimo, -a; décimo primeiro	Ordinal numbers
2nd	segundo, -a	12th	duodécimo, -a; décimo segundo	
3rd	terceiro, -a	13th	décimo terceiro	
4th	quarto, -a	20th	vigésimo, -a	
5th	quinto, -a	21st	vigésimo primeiro, -a	
6th	sexto, -a	30th	trigésimo, -a	
7th	sétimo, -a	40th	quadragésimo, -a	
8th	oitavo, -a	50th	quinquagésimo, -a	
9th	nono, -a	60th	sexuagésimo, -a	
10th	décimo, -a	100th	centésimo, -a	

Men are usually addressed as "o Senhor", women as "minha Senhora". Forms of address
If you know a man's name you should address him by his name with the
prefix "o Senhor"; younger women, particularly if they are unmarried,
are addressed by their Christian name with the prefix "a Senhora", older
ladies only by Senhora Dona and their Christian name. "You" in direct
address is "o Senhor", "a Senhora" or "Vossê", in the plural "os
Senhores", "as Senhoras" or "Vocês".

Good morning, good day	Bom dia	Idioms
Good afternoon	Boa tarde	
Good evening, good night	Boa noite	
Goodbye	Adeus, Até à vista	
Yes, no	Sim, não	
Excuse me (apologising)	Desculpe, Perdão	
Excuse me (e.g. when passing in front of someone)	Com licença	
After you (e.g. offering something)	A vontade!	
Please (asking for something)	Faz favor	
Thank you (very much)	(Muito) obrigado	
Not at all (You're welcome)	De nada, Não tem de què	
How are you?	Como está?	
Very well	Muíto bem	

Do you speak English?	O senhor fala inglês?
A little, not much	Um pouco, não muito
I don't understand	Não comprendo (nada)
What is the Portuguese for...?	Como se diz em português...?

Have you got a room?	Tem um quarto livre?	In the hotel
How much is it?	Quanto custa?	
breakfast	pequenho almoço o café da manhã	
lunch	almoço	
dinner	o jantar	
half board	meia pensão	
full board	a pensão completa	
everything included	tudo incluído	
bill, please!	faz favor, a conta!	
Please make out the bill	Prepare me a conta, se faz favor	

See Food and Drink	Madeiran menu

Where is ... the nearest taxi rank?	Pode-me dizer, se faz favor, onde é a praça de táxis mais próxima?	Getting about
To the station, please	Para a estação, por favor	
To the hotel, please	Para o hotel, por favor	
To the airport, please	para o aeroporto	

Language

To ..., please	Para ..., se faz favor
tourist information	poste de turismo
filling station	posto de gasolina
supermarket	supermercado
Please stop here	Pare aqui, por favor
How much is it to ...?	Quanto terei de pagar para ir até ...?
Do you have anything to declare?	Tem alguma coisa a declarar?
passport	o passaporte
identity card	o bilhete de identidade
right, left	á direita, esquerda
straight ahead	sempre a direito
above, below	em cima, em baixo
how far?	que distância?
Where is the toilet?	Quarto de banho, faz favor?
ladies/gents	senhoras/senhores

Road signs

Alto	Stop
Atenção	Look out
Cuidado	Go carefully
Perigo	Danger
Devagar	Slow down
Auto-estrada	Motorway
Curva perigosa	Dangerous bend
Dê passagem	Give way
Proibido ultrapassar	No overtaking
Passagem proibida	No entry
Obras, Trabalhos	Road works
Desvio	Diversion
Direcção única; Sentido único	One-way street
Estacionamento proibido	Parking prohibited
Parque de estacionamento	Car park, parking place
Policia	Police

Out and about

east	leste	west	oeste
south	sul	north	norte
hill	monte	valley	vale
town	cidade	village	aldeia
street	estrada	road	caminho
avenue	avenida	bairro	quarter
beach	praia	sea	mar
river	rio	cliffs	rocha
port	porto	lighthouse	farol
church	igreja	museum	museu
cathedral	sé	tower	torre
market	mercado	house	casa
country house	quinta	courtyard	pátio
viewpoint	mirador	round trip	circulação

Months

January	janeiro	July	julho
February	fevereiro	August	agosto
March	março	September	setembro
April	abril	October	outubro
May	maio	November	novembro
June	junho	December	dezembro

Monday	segunda-feira	Days of the week
Tuesday	terça-feira	
Wednesday	quarta-feira	
Thursday	quinta-feira	
Friday	sexta-feira	
Saturday	sábado	
Sunday	domingo	

New Year's Day	Ano Novo	Holidays and feastdays
Carnival	o Carnaval	
Shrove Tuesday	Terça-Feira de Cinzas	
Ash Wednesday	Quarta-Feira de Cinzas	
Good Friday	Sexta-Feira Santa	
Easter	Páscoa	
Ascension	Ascensão	
Whitsun	Espírito Santo, Pentecostes	
April 25th (Liberation Day)	Dia da Liberdade	
May 1st	primeiro de Maio	
Corpus Christi	Corpo de Deus	
June 10th (Portugal Day)	Feriad Nacional	
All Saints	Todos de Santos	
Christmas Eve	consoada	
Christmas	o Natal	
New Year's Eve	a passagem do ano	

Head post office	a estação central dos correios	At the post office
Where is the nearest post office?	Onde é o correio mais próximo?	
... the nearest letterbox?	... a caixa de correio mais próximo?	
collection	a tiragem	
By airmail please	Queria mandar esta carta por avião	
How much does this letter cost?	Quanto é que se paga para uma carta?	
How much does this postcard cost?	Quanto é que se paga para uma postal?	
stamp	selo	
express letter	carta por expresso	

I should like to make a phone call	Eu queria uma chamada para, se faz favor	Telephoning
Hello, who's that?	Está? Quem fala?	
Can I speak to Mr/Mrs	Posso falar com o senhor/a senhora	
.... please	... se faz favor?	
phone call	chamada	
international call	chamada internacional	
dialling code	indicativo	
telephone exchange	a central telefónica	
telegram	telegrama	

Libraries

Madeira has a number of libraries where information about the island's history is available.

Funchal's Municipal Library (Bibliotecas Municipais) in the town hall's Museu da Cidade is a fund of information on local history (tel. 22 28 49). The library in the natural history museum (Museu Municipal) can also be used by prior appointment (tel. 22 97 61). The Barbeito library (48 Avenida Arriaga) has a large store of books on Christopher Columbus, while the Biblioteca Calouste Gulbenkian (Avenida Arriaga; tel. 22 72 51) caters for reading on more general themes.

Lost Property

Madeira has no official lost property office but the police station in Funchal at Rua João de Deus (tel. 22 20 22), keeps any lost property that is handed in. It can also supply an official form for the insurance company if missing items are not recovered. In any case if anything of value is lost report it to the nearest police station or police officer.

Maps

Large-scale maps to supplement the one that accompanies this guide are widely available from most good bookshops. These maps include, in Britain, the Bartholomew Holiday Map and, in Madeira, those of the Instituto Geográfico e Cadastral. Local maps, including a free map of Madeira and Funchal, are available from the Funchal tourist office (see Information) and the island's bookshops, etc. Walking tour maps, levada trails, etc. also feature in John and Pat Underwood's "Landscapes of Madeira" (see Recommended Reading).

Markets

Flower markets

Funchal market, the two-storey Mercado dos Lavradores fronting Ribeira de João Gomes, is at its busiest on Fridays and Saturdays. Here as well as every kind of fish, fruit and vegetable, all the flowers which are such a feature of Madeira are on sale. To take flowers home make sure they are properly packaged and labelled for air travel.

There is also a little flower market of long-standing behind Funchal Cathedral and its flower sellers, who by law have to wear traditional Madeiran costume, will gladly make up bouquets from the blooms of your choice.

Gipsy market

The Gipsy market in Funchal's Old Town quarter (Zona Velha) is a street market full of traders of all kinds.

Warning – remember when buying clothes the quality is not always what you would expect from the label.

Media

Newspapers and periodicals

Most English and American newspapers and periodicals are on sale at hotels and newsagents within a day or two of publication. The Madeira Island Bulletin, which publishes what's on locally, is a free monthly paper in English and is available from Funchal's tourist office.

Radio

Radio Turista, Madeira's Tourist Radio, broadcasts a daily programme in English on weekdays between 5.45 and 6.30pm on 1485 medium wave. It is also possible to get the BBC World Service, Voice of America, and Radio Canada International on short wave.

Television

There are four channels on Portuguese television, the two state-run channels (RTP 1 and 2) and TVI and SIC. Foreign films are usually shown in the original language with sub-titles. Most hotels also have satellite TV which picks up English-language programmes and screens major sporting events.

Medical Care

Madeira has quite good health care facilities although its only hospitals are in Funchal. Outside the capital almost everywhere has a health centre (Centro do Saúde) and in some cases – Ribeira Brava, Calheta, São Vicente, Porto Moniz, Santana, Machico and, on Porto Santo, Vila Baleira – these also have their own casualty units. In extreme emergencies go to the nearest doctor for treatment. The tourist offices can supply you with a list of doctors and dentists who speak English.

Health care facilities

Treatment is free for EU residents with form E111. Without this patients have to pay for treatment at the time and then claim it back on travel insurance. It is advisable to take out travel insurance in any case as this also covers the cost of return travel home if necessary.

Treatment costs

Outpatient treatment of minor ailments and injuries can be received at the Centro Médico da Sé at 42 Rua dos Murcos (tel. 23 01 27/23 17 79-82). See also below and Emergency Services.

Minor casualties

See entry

Chemists

See entry

Emergency services

Hospitals and Clinics

Clínica de Santa Catarina (24-hr. outpatient department)
115 Rua 5 de Outubro; tel. 74 11 50

In Funchal

Hospital Cruz de Carvalho
Av. Luís de Camões; tel. 74 11 11/73 21 11

Hospital Dr João de Almada
Quinta Santana (Monte); tel. 22 57 71

Clínica de Santa Luzia (24-hr outpatient department)
5 Rua da Torrinha; tel. 23 34 34

Clínica Dentária Cinco de Outubro (dental clinic)
79a Rua 5 de Outubro; tel. 22 82 17
For dental emergencies on Sundays and holidays contact:
Medicina Dentária, Serviço de Urgência (tel. 22 25 80)

On Porto Santo
Centro de Saúde de Porto Santo, Rua do Penedo; tel. 98 22 11

Motoring

When driving on Madeira's often narrow and twisting country roads take great care and be constantly alert, especially if unfamiliar with the terrain. The road network as a whole, though, is currently being upgraded and extended as part of a programme funded by the European Union.

Madeiran roads

On Madeira – as in the rest of Portugal – vehicles travel on the right and overtake on the left.

Drive on the right

Temporary road closures due to rockfalls, landslides, etc., after spells of bad weather are very much a possibility to be reckoned with. There is

Road closures

usually no alternative but to turn round and go back the way you came –
carrying on regardless could be very dangerous.

When driving on Madeira's narrow coastal roads one main rule to remember is when meeting oncoming traffic it is the driver nearest a passing place who should wait or reverse. The usual European road signs
apply.

Rules of the road

If the car breaks down, the many bends in Madeira's roads make it absolutely vital to alert other traffic by putting out warning triangles as quickly
as possible.

Warning triangle

The breath-test limit for alcohol in the blood is 0.5 millilitre. The wisest
course, though, is not to drink and drive.

Breath-test

The wearing of seat-belts is compulsory and children under 12 are only
allowed to sit in the back. Although many of the locals apparently ignore
the law the nature of Madeira's roads makes it all the more important to
wear a seat-belt, even at low speeds. Motorcyclists must wear a helmet.

Seat-belts and
helmets for
motorcyclists

The speed limit for cars and motorcycles is 50kph in built-up areas and
90kph elsewhere.

Speed limits

Funchal has plenty of filling stations but they are harder to find elsewhere
on the island, so for long journeys fill up before setting out.

Filling stations

When hiring a car find out which garages to go to in the event of a breakdown and what procedures to follow.
   Madeira has no automobile club but there are garages with repair
shops in all the main places.

Breakdown
assistance

See Travel Documents

Vehicle papers

See entry .

Insurance

Museums

Nearly all Madeira's museums are in Funchal and several of them are well
worth a visit to learn more about the island's history. They are usually
open during the week but closed at weekends and on Mondays. For
precise details of opening times see under the entry for the individual
museum in the A to Z section.

Madeira Wine Company
A good exhibition on Madeira wine with many old wine-making artefacts
and an opportunity to taste some Madeira.

Museums
in Funchal

Photographia Museu Vicentes
Vicente Gomes da Silva was Portugal's first ever public photographer and
this charming little museum of photography is in his original studio
which dates from 1848. Besides viewing the quaint equipment there are
also albums of historic photographs of Madeira's past to look at.

◄ *The stylish taste of the former owner can be seen in the
Winter Garden of the Museu Frederico de Freitas*

Music

Club Sport Maritimo
This is the place for sports fans keen on checking out an amazing variety
of unusual cups and other sporting trophies.

Fortaleza de São Tiago (Museu de Arte Contemporânea)
This museum of contemporary art is housed in the Fortaleza de São
Tiago, a picturesque 17th c. fort.

Museu da Cidade
Housed in Funchal Town Hall (Câmara Municipal), this little museum
documents the town's history.

Museu de Arte Sacra
One of Funchal's most important museums, its sacred art includes Portugal's finest works by 15th and 16th c. Flemish masters.

Museu Municipal
A natural history museum with an aquarium on the ground floor and a
fascinating collection of fossils and stuffed animals and sea creatures.

Casa Museu Frederico de Freitas
The large collection of works of art, antique furniture and everyday
domestic utensils bequeathed by lawyer Frederico de Freitas can be seen
on display in his elegant 18th c. house.

Quinta das Cruzes
The collection of fine antiques housed in this beautifully restored 18th/
19th c. quinta reflect Madeira's cultural history, as does its archaeological
garden containing pieces of stonework from all over the island.

Museu do Vinho
Like the headquarters of the Madeira Wine Company, the wine museum
on Rue 5 de Outubro shows in detail how Madeira's very own famous
wine is made (Open: Mon.–Fri. 9.30–12 and 2–5pm).

Museu do Bombeiro
Funchal's interesting little fire brigade museum on Estrada Luso-
Brasileiro tells the story of Madeiran firefighting (Open: Sun. 9am–1pm).

I.B.T.A.M. Museum
Madeira's Institute of Embroidery, Tapestry and Handicrafts showcases
the local handicrafts in an exhibition which includes some very old pieces
(Open: Mon.–Fri. 9–12.30 and 2–5.30pm).

Museum in
Caniçal
Caniçal's little whaling museum, the Museu da Baleia, tells the history of
whaling on Madeira but also makes the case for whale conservation, including Save the Whale pictures by children from around the world.

Music

Folklore
Many hotels, such as the Savoy, stage regular evenings of Madeiran folklore for their guests. Some restaurants also have folk dancing evenings
where the dancers in their traditional costumes perform to the music of
Madeiran instruments such as the machête and the brinquinho.

Madeira Music
Festival
Madeira's annual Music Festival takes place in Funchal in June. Details of
where to get tickets for this highly acclaimed festival, with its international orchestras and celebrity soloists, can be obtained from the Funchal
tourist office (see Information).

Many festivals on Madeira are religious or traditional, with musicians going from house to house

Newspapers and Periodicals

See Media

Nightlife

Most of Madeira's nightlife is to be found in Funchal and the Hotel Zone, where plenty of the hotels have nightclubs and bars, some of them with discos as well. The Casino Park Hotel on Rua Imperatriz Dona Amélia puts on three evening shows a week; tickets are obtainable from hotel reception.

Madeira's nightlife centres on Funchal

Funchal's most popular discos include "O Farol" in the Madeira Carlton Hotel and "Formula 1" at 5 Rua do Favilha. Another favourite with tourists and locals alike is "Refléx" (Travessa da Praça) which stays open every night till 5am.

Discos

Funchal Old Town (Zona Velha) has plenty of bars where there is no problem mingling with the Madeirans. Among the top popular venues are Berilights (cnr. Estrada Monumental/Rua do Gorgulho), Salsa Latina (Rua da Imperatriz D. Amélia) and Number Two (Rua do Favilha). Popular bars in the Hotel Zone include the cheery Local Bar (25 Rua Casa Branca) and, just down the road at No. 62, the White House Pub and Restaurant.

Bars

Madeira's only casino is in the grounds of the Casino Park Hotel. It has the usual roulette, blackjack, bingo, etc., as well as its share of one-armed

Casino

163

bandits. To gain admission visitors must be over 21, produce their passport or identity card, and be dressed appropriately.

Opening Times

Official bodies	Mon.–Fri. 8am–12 and 1.30–4pm
Shops	Mon.–Fri. 8.30–12.30 and 2–6pm. Some shops in Funchal stay open during the lunch hour and/or keep open later at night.
Banks	See Money
Chemists	See entry
Museums	See entry
Post offices	See Post and Telecommunications

Post and Telecommunications

Post
Post offices
The Portuguese for post – Correio – is also the sign for a post office.

Opening hours
Post offices are usually open Mon.–Fri. from 9–12.30 and 2.30–6.30pm. The main post office in Funchal is open for longer i.e. Mon.–Fri. 8.30am–8pm and Sat. 9am–1pm. Telephone calls can be made from here until 10pm.
   The post office in the Hotel Zone (318 Estrada Monumental, in the Lido Sol supermarket) is open 9am–7pm but closed on Saturdays.

Postage
The postage for ordinary letters (cartas) and postcards (postais) within Europe is 75 Esc., and the airmail rate is 350 Esc. Stamps (selos) can be obtained from post offices (correios) and in shops with the sign "CTT Selos".

Letter boxes
Most letter boxes are red and they can be either pillar-boxes or mailboxes on walls.

Poste restante
Poste restante mail should be labelled "posta restante" and sent to the appropriate post office. A passport is needed when collecting letters.

Telegrams
Telegrams (telegrama) can be sent from all the larger post offices, or handed in at hotel front desks.

Fax
Madeira has plenty of fax facilities. Most hotels also have their own fax machines and will be able to send faxes for guests.

Telephone
Most of Madeira's public telephones take phonecards rather than coins. These phonecards (Cartão Credifone) can be bought from most post offices, from Portuguese Telecom direct, or shops with a Telecom sign. They are for 50 or 120 units (750/1800 Esc. respectively). Calls can also be made from the main post office.

International calls
For international calls from Portugal via the operator dial 099 for Europe and 098 for elsewhere. For direct dialling, the country codes are as follows:

To Portugal:
00 351, then the area code minus the first 0, i.e. 91 for Madeira, then the number

From Portugal:
Canada: 00 1 (then as calls for Madeira)
United Kingdom: 00 44
United States: 00 1

Useful numbers
Directory enquiries (for Madeira): 118
Weather forecast: 150 (in Portuguese)

Public Holidays

See Festivals and Holidays

Public Transport

Madeira has such a good bus network that it is easy to get to almost anywhere on the island by public transport.

The Portuguese for bus is "autocarro", and a bus-stop is "paragem". **Buses**

Information on bus services is available from the Bom Jesus shopping   Information
centre in Rua 31 de Janeiro and from the tourist office.

Line 1   Funchal–Ponte dos Frades–Funchal   **Bus lines**
            (via Vila de Cámara de Lobos)

Line 2   Funchal–Assomada/Caniço–Funchal

Line 3   Funchal–Castelejo–Funchal
            (via Estreito de Cámara de Lobos)

Line 4   Funchal–Madalena do Mar–Funchal
            (via Estreito de Cámara de Lobos, Ribeira Brava and Ponta do
            Sol)

Line 6   Funchal–Boaventura
            (via Estreito de Cámara de Lobos, Ribeira Brava, Serra
            D'Agua, Encumeada, São Vicente and Ponta Delgada)

Line 7   Funchal–Ribeira Brava–Funchal

Line 20   Funchal–Santo da Serra
            (via Santa Catarina airport and Machico)

Line 27   Funchal–Caldeira–Funchal
            (via Vila de Cámara de Lobos)

Line 29   Funchal–Camacha–Funchal

Line 53   Funchal–Fajal–Funchal
            (via Santa Catarina airport and Ribeiro de Machico)

Line 56   Funchal–Porto da Cruz–Funchal
            (via Monte, Poiso and Santo Roque Faial)

Line 60   Boqueirão Santa Cruz–Funchal
            (via Gaula)

Line 77   Funchal–Santo da Serra–Funchal

Line 78   Funchal–Faial–Funchal
(via Santa Catarina airport and Machico)

Line 80   Porto Moniz–Funchal
(via São Vicente, Encumeada, Ribeira Brava and Estreito de
Cámara de Lobos)
To get from Funchal to Porto Moniz take bus no.139

Line 81   Funchal–Curral das Freiras–Funchal

Line 96   Funchal–Corticeiras/Jardim da Serra–Funchal
(via Estreito de Cámara de Lobos)

Line 103   Funchal–Boaventura–Funchal
(via Monte, Poiso, Cruzinhas, Faial, Santana, São Jorge, Arco
de Jorge)

Line 107   Funchal–Ponta do Pargo–Funchal
(via Estreito de Cámara de Lobos, Ribeira Brava, Canhas,
Estrela Calheta, Prazeres, Ponta do Pargo and Santa)

Line 113   Funchal–Caniçal–Funchal
(via Santa Catarina airport)

Line 132   Santana–São Vicente–Santana
(via São Jorge, Arco São Jorge, Fajá do Penedo, Boaventura
and Ponta Delgada)

Line 136   Funchal–Vargem–Funchal
(via Garajau)

Line 138   Funchal–Cabanas–Funchal
(via Monte, Poiso, Cruzinhas, Faial, Santana and São Jorge)

Line 139   Funchal–Porto Moniz–Funchal
(via Estreito de Cámara de Lobos, Ribeira Brava, Encumeada
and São Vicente)
To get back to Funchal you take bus no. 80!

Line 142   Funchal–Ponta do Pargo
(via Estreito de Cámara de Lobos, Ribeira Brava, Canhas,
Estrela da Calheta and Prazeres)

Line 148   Funchal–Boa Morte–Funchal
via Estreito de Cámara de Lobos)

Line 155   Funchal–Ponta da Oliveira–Funchal

Line 156   Funchal–Maroços–Funchal
(via Machico)

Taxis   See entry

Radio and Television

See Media

Recommended Reading

For further reading about Madeira there are plenty of books on the subject in any good bookshop. The following suggestions give some idea of the range on offer:

Underwood, Pat and John: *The Madeira Book*; Sunflower Books, London (1994)

Underwood, Pat and John: *Landscapes of Madeira*; Sunflower Books, London (5th edition 1997)

Don Glen Sandy: *Madeira Wine at Home*; Empresa do Bolhão, Porto (1988)

H.J.Weaver: *Reid's Hotel – Jewel of the Atlantic*; Island Hotel Ltd., Funchal (1991)

Restaurants

Despite the half a million visitors who eat out here every year Madeira has managed to retain much of its culinary individuality, and, aside from the inevitable concessions to global tourism, its restaurant menus still largely consist of traditional local fare. As you would expect of an island people the Madeirans are particularly good at fish dishes, including "espada" to name just one typical speciality.

Local
Madeiran cuisine

The pleasant climate all year enables outdoor eating at many places – Funchal's Old Town has a number of particularly attractive restaurants in this category.

Menus are usually in English as well as Portuguese.

Menus

A three-course meal will usually cost between 2,200 and 3,500 Esc. per person, not including drinks and coffee. Some of the more expensive restaurants also add a cover charge.

Prices

Early reservation is advisable for the more expensive restaurants.

Reservations

See entry

Tipping

Restaurants in Funchal (selection)

Restaurante and Bar "Adega A Cuba", 28 Rua do Bispo; tel. 22 09 86. Striking rustic decor, close to the centre. Superb sandwiches and light meals. Open: daily 8am–10pm.

Madeiran cuisine

Restaurante "Arsénio's", 169 Rua de Santa Maria (in the old town); tel. 2 40 07. Speciality: espetada (charcoal-grilled beef kebab). Open: daily 10am–11pm.

Restaurante "Casa Madeirense", 153 Estrada Monumental; tel. 76 67 00. Speciality: fish dishes. Open: daily 11am–11pm.

Restaurante "Le Jardin", Rua D. Carlos (in the old town); tel. 22 28 64. Specialities: flambé dishes. Open: daily 10am–midnight.

Restaurante "Montanha", 101 Estrada Nacional, Neves de São Gonçalo; tel. 79 31 82. This restaurant on the edge of the town centre deserves a special mention for its wonderful view over Funchal harbour. Grilled dishes are a speciality. Book early to get a window table.

Restaurante "O Almirante", Largo Poço (in the old town); tel. 22 42 52/22 56 73. Specialities: fish, seafood, crustaceans, kebabs. Open: daily 10am–11pm.

Restaurante "O Tapassol", 1 Rua D. Carlos (in the old town); tel. 22 50 23. Specialities: espada (fish), espetada (meat kebabs). Open: daily 10am–11pm.

Restaurante "Vagrant", Avenida do Mar (moored in the harbour); tel. 22 35 72. Unique restaurant on board a yacht built for an American millionaire in the Forties and owned by the Beatles for a time in the Sixties before it finally ended up in Funchal harbour. Specialities: fish and seafood. Open: daily 11.30am–3.30pm and 6–11.30pm.

By the Marina   The many little restaurants lining the Marina stay open from about 10am until late in the evening and cater primarily for tourists. They also serve typical Madeiran food and sometimes have folk dancing.

International   "Le Faunes" (in Reid's Hotel), 139 Estrada Monumental; tel. 7 00 07 71 71. Probably Madeira's best restaurant, gourmet international cuisine with a regional input. Expensive but good value, if only for the fascinating view of Funchal. Open: daily 7.30–11pm except Sundays (reservation definitely recommended).

Restaurante "Carochinha", 2a Rua de São Francisco; tel. 22 36 95. Speciality: English fare (roast beef, steaks). Open: daily noon–10pm (Sat. 12–3pm and 6–10pm).

Restaurante "Casa dos Reis", 6 Rua da Penha de França; tel. 22 51 82. Specialities: Portuguese and French cuisine. Open: daily 7am–10.30pm.

Italian   Trattoria "Villa Cliff" (near Reid's Hotel), 139 Estrada Monumental; tel. 7 00 70 79. Superb view of Funchal. Specialities: pasta. Open: daily 11am–2pm and 7–11pm.

Restaurants outside Funchal (selection)

Calheta   Restaurante "Costa Verde"; tel. 82 34 22. Recommended for its grilled beef but good fish dishes as well. Open: daily 10am–2am.

Curral das Freiras (Valley of Nuns)   Restaurante "Casa de Abrigo do Poiso"; tel. 78 22 69. Speciality: smoked or grilled trout. Open: daily 11am–11pm.

Restaurante "Nun Valley", in the village centre; tel. 71 21 77. Good Madeiran food. Bottles of this restaurant's speciality – it distills its own liqueur – are on sale. Open: daily 10am–10pm.

Estreito Camara de Lobos   Restaurante "Santo António", Quinta Santo Antonio; tel. 94 54 39/94 75 86. Specialities: espetada, spit-roast chicken, salt cod. Open: daily 11am–11pm. Telephone reservation recommended.

Ponta do Sol   Restaurante "A Capoeira", Sítio da Igreja; tel. 94 52 26/94 66 80. Speciality: meat grills. Open: daily 11am–midnight.

Restaurante and Bar "Cancela"; tel. 97 27 36. Popular with locals as well as tourists. Specialities: beef dishes such as espetada.

Restaurante "Casa de Pasto", Sítio Chão da Ribeira (Seixal); tel. 85 45 59/ **Porto Moniz**
85 44 70. This restaurant still serves espetada made the traditional way,
with the meat skewered on a bay twig suspended above the table, and
the diners helping themselves to their portion. Open: daily 11am–
10.30pm.

Restaurante "Agua Mar"; tel. 95 11 48. Specialities: freshly caught fish, **Ribeira Brava**
crustaceans. Open: daily 9am–11pm.

Restaurante "Vista Alegre", 101 Estrada Regional (Pinheiro); tel. 95 36 14/
95 37 65. Speciality: espada fillets, espetada, grills. Open: daily noon–
11pm except Mon.

Scuba Diving

See Sport

Shopping and Souvenirs

Madeira's shopping quarter is in Funchal town centre and the area **Shopping quarter**
around the cathedral. There are also many stores and a shopping mall
full of boutiques in the Hotel Zone.

The Casa do Turista (Rua do Conseilheiro) is a department store on the Casa do Turista
seafront which stocks the whole range of typical Madeiran handicrafts

*One of the many shops in Funchal with a wide selection of attractive
and tasteful souvenirs*

and other products. This is a good place to browse and find out what Madeira has to offer in the way of souvenirs.

Needlework

One of the classic souvenirs for many visitors is the traditional embroidery. Besides lacework and other forms of needlework, tapestry scenes such as copies of the works of Old Masters are to be found. To make sure that a purchase is a genuine Madeiran product look for the lead seal of the I.B.T.A.M., the Institute of Madeiran Embroidery, Tapestry and Handicrafts.

Visits can be arranged to some of Funchal's 50 plus workshops and their showrooms to see how the goods are made. For further details contact the tourist office in Funchal (see Information).

Wickerwork is another popular but conceivably much bulkier souvenir. However to take home a really big item, such as a piece of furniture, size need not pose a problem since the Café Relógio in Camacha, where the wickerwork comes from, can arrange shipment and complete all the formalities.

Flowers

The same applies to blooms such as orchids, bird of paradise flowers, etc. Shops such as those in Funchal's Mercado dos Lavradores and the Quinta Boavista will box them up and label them so that they will arrive home in good condition.

Madeira wine

See Food and Drink

Other typical souvenirs

One Madeiran souvenir like no other is the "brinquinho". This is a percussion instrument with a difference – a kind of miniature maypole carrying little dolls in traditional costume which keep the beat by clashing together their bells and castanets when they are moved up and down the pole. Other souvenirs of a more practical nature include the traditional kid-skin boots and woollen hats and cardigans.

Books

The Livraria "O Pátio" in the courtyard of the Vicente Photography Museum (Rua da Carreira) stocks a good range of books on Madeiran life, history and culture.

Opening times

See entry

Sport

Funchal tourist office (see Information) can supply leaflets giving details of all the sports facilities on Madeira.

Angling

See entry

Football

Like all the Portuguese the Madeirans love their football, whether as players – the island now has many more pitches than it used to – or spectators. Since their team Club Sport Maritimo is in Portugal's first division they are able to see top fixtures such as Benfica Lisbon versus FC Porto. Home games are played in Funchal's Estádio dos Barreiros, Madeira's biggest stadium (north of the Hotel Zone on Rua Dr. Pita). For fixture details check the local press or ask at hotel reception.

Golf

Madeira has two golf courses considered to be amongst Europe's finest and most spectacular. Non-members can use them on payment of the green fees; clubs, etc. can also be hired.

Palheiro Golf (in the grounds of the Quinta do Palheiro; 18 holes)
Information and bookings: tel. 79 21 16, fax. 79 24 56
Outstanding for its superb views of Funchal

*The golf course at Quinta do Paleiro: the many courses on Madeira
are among the best in Europe*

Santa da Serra (27 holes)
Information and bookings: tel. 55 23 45, fax. 55 23 67
This is the course for the annual Madeira Open in January which
attracts some of the world's top golfers.

Aeroclub da Madeira
Rua do Castanheiro (Funchal)   Hang-gliding
tel. 22 83 11, fax 22 12 65

Eurofun¬Navio Azul
Estrada Monumental (Funchal)
tel. 76 16 84, fax 6 16 93

Terras da Aventura and Turismo
25 Caminho do Amparo (Funchal)
tel. 3 38 18/6 10 18, fax 6 10 18

For information about horse riding on Madeira contact: Horse riding

Centro Hipismo da Madeira
Caminho dos Pretos (Funchal); tel. 79 29 10/79 25 82

For information about cross-country riding, etc. on Porto Santo contact:

Centro Hípico do Porto Santo
Quinta dos Profetas (Sítio da Ponta); tel. 98 31 65

Escola de Equitação J.C.C.
Campo de Baixo; tel. 98 27 41

Sport

Jogging
There is a jogging track along a signed trail in Quinta Magnólia park (Rua do Dr Pita).

Keep-fit
The larger hotels have fitness suites with all the necessary equipment and, in some cases, qualified trainers. These facilities are also open to non-residents for what is usually quite a small fee. To find out which hotels offer this enquire at reception.

Sailing, wind-surfing, canoeing
Some hotels in Funchal rent out sail-boards, small sailing boats and canoes. If stasying at a hotel which does not, try one of the following:

Associação Nautica da Madeira
Posto publico – Marina do Funchal (Funchal)
tel. 4 99 89

Associação Regional de Vela e Canoagem
São Lázaro, Marina do Funchal (Funchal)
tel. 22 49 70

Centro de Treino de Mar da Madeira
São Lázaro, Marina do Funchal (Funchal)
tel. 23 08 25, fax 23 11 77

Club Naval do Funchal
Barração de actividades Náuticas
São Lázaro, Marina do Funchal (Funchal)
tel. 22 46 61, fax 22 57 33

Scuba-diving and snorkelling
The waters of the Atlantic around Madeira and Porto Santo are among the most exciting for snorkelling and scuba-diving. Some companies specialise in underwater expeditions, equipment rental and diving courses. These include:

Club Naval do Funchal
Barração de actividades Náuticas
São Lázaro, Marina do Funchal (Funchal)
tel. 22 46 61, fax 22 57 33

Scorpio Divers
Complexo Balnear do Lido (in Funchal lido)
tel. 6 69 77, fax 22 50 20

Manta-Reiner
Caniço
tel. 93 46 11/2 or 94 40 20, fax 93 46 80

Urs Moser Diving Center
5 Rua J.G.Zarco (Funchal)
tel. 4 49 89

Squash
Many hotels have squash courts, but if not there are several at the leisure complex in Quinta Magnólia park.

Swimming
See Bathing Beaches, Swimming

Tennis
All the larger hotels have their own tennis courts, some of them floodlit. Public courts, with floodlighting, are also for hire in Quinta Magnólia park.

Walking
See entry

Swimming

The large hotels in and around Funchal have their own access to sea-bathing. This is usually free for residents but some allow non-residents to use their facilities and charge admission.

    For a small fee sea-bathing is possible at the Club Naval do Funchal and the Club de Turismo, both on Estrada Monumental, while at the eastern end of Funchal Old Town, sea-bathing is free below the Fortaleza de São Tiago.

Sea-bathing

Nearly all Madeira's hotels have their own swimming pools, most of them heated. Families with children but no hotel pool will find the large Lido complex on Rua Gorgulho a welcome alternative. It is relatively cheap, has two main pools and a children's pool, plus rocks and terraces by the sea for sunbathing. There is a small charge for sunbeds and sunshades. The public pool in Quinta Magnólia is another good one for families with children.

Swimming pools

See entry

Bathing beaches

Taxis

Madeira's taxis (mostly quite smart Volvos and Mercedes) are yellow with a blue stripe, and those that have been approved by the tourist office have a "T" on the windscreen. The drivers have formed themselves into a co-operative which has had the advantage of standardising fares.

To telephone for a taxi the numbers to call – from anywhere in Funchal – are: tel. 2 22 09 11, 22 20 00 and 22 25 00. Since every taxi has a radio-telephone, there is usually very little delay before one arrives.

Taxis by telephone

Taxi ranks in the centre of Funchal are to be found on Rua D. Carlos, Avenida do Mar, Rua de Sante, in the Hotel Zone, etc. Outside the capital any place of any size has a rank close to the bus stops or in the centre.

Taxi ranks

The standard fare inside Funchal is currently 300 Esc. for the first 120 metres plus 20 Esc. for every additional 60 metres. It has become customary to round the total fare up to the next full stage.

Fares

Every taxi has to carry a notice giving the standard prices for cross-country journeys, but it is possible to negotiate a special deal to hire the taxi for a number of trips on different days. The standard amount for a whole day is currently 15,000 Esc. The taxi-drivers' co-operative publishes a leaflet giving the prices for various whole- and half-day tours of Madeira.

Cross-country journeys

Complaints should be made to the Taxi Co-operative (tel. 22 04 92), who will also need to know the vehicle registration or the driver's licence number.

Complaints

See entry

Tipping

Telephone

See Post and Telecommunications

Time

Madeira, like the rest of Portugal, observes Greenwich Mean Time (GMT) plus one hour in winter and GMT plus two hours in summer, i.e. from April to November.

Tipping

Hotels

Like anywhere else, it is customary to give a tip for good service. For hotel maids the tip for a week is about 1000 Esc.

Restaurants

Service is included but the usual practice is to round up the amount on the bill.

Porters

Airport and hotel porters normally expect a small tip.

Taxi-drivers

Taxi drivers are also used to having the fare rounded upwards or being allowed to keep the change.

Travel Documents

Personal
documents

Visitors to Madeira from EU countries, including Ireland and the UK, and from Australia, Canada, New Zealand and the United States only require a valid passport, and can stay for up to 60 days without a visa. Children under 16 must either have their own passport or be entered in one of their parent's passports.

It is always a good idea to take a photocopy of your passport and two passport photographs to facilitate getting a replacement in the event of loss.

Driving licence

To hire a car all that is needed is a national driving licence.

Walking

Madeira is a
great place
for walkers

Anyone who visits Madeira without taking at least one walk along the levadas cannot say they have really seen the island. Even the most experienced walkers enthuse about the unique beauty of the landscape which awaits them on a simple excursion into the countryside.

Travel Agents organise a variety of programmes for walks, mountaineering and mountain biking. Also, Walking and Nature Reserve Programmes are offered by:
Eurofun
Navio Azul Shopping Centre
Estrada Monumental, Funchal
Tel. 22 86 38, Fax. 22 86 20

Terras de Adventura and Turismo
Caminho do Amparo No. 25, Funchal
Tel. 61018, Fax. 61018

Recommended
walks

There are a number of recommended walks and trails in the A to Z section under the relevant destinations. For a detailed and very informative guide to all of Madeira's levada walks in all kinds of conditions the most highly recommended publication is "Landscapes of Madeira" by John and Pat Underwood (Sunflower Books, 5th edition 1997).

For walking along one of the well-signed paths all that is needed is sensible footwear with soles which have a good grip. Longer excursions along the levadas call for proper walking boots, waterproofs, protection against the sun, etc. Remember that the weather can change very suddenly, especially in the mountains, and walkers without the right equipment could run into real danger. If going on one of the levada walks through tunnels take a torch and check that it has a broad enough beam to take in both the floor and the roof.

What to take

Before going walking in the mountains or embarking on a long levada trek it is important to find out locally what kind of weather is expected. If warned against setting out, take it seriously and do not go. Sudden changes in the weather can make venturing out very dangerous. June should be avoided for a walking holiday as this is when the mountains are usually shrouded in mist.

Warning

If walking alone be sure to leave details of your route with someone before setting out.

Weather Forecasting

The very latest weather forecast in Portuguese is obtainable by telephone (tel. 150).

It is possible, however, to do some amateur forecasting by keeping an eye on what is happening to the Desertas, the islands to the southeast of the main island. If they can be seen clearly then the eastern parts of Madeira will be clear, with cloud in the west. If the Desertas are covered in cloud and the wind is from the north-east, the western parts of Madeira will be clear while the eastern side will probably be cloudy. If the Desertas are barely visible and the wind is blowing from the north-east it is highly likely that the cloud is only in the south of Madeira. This is the best time to go walking in the mountains.

The Desertas are also a good indicator of general weather conditions. If they appear to be very close and to have a hazy white line on the horizon rain is most probably in the offing.

When to Go

See Facts and Figures, Climate (p.12)

Climate

Because of its extremely pleasant climate all the year round a visit to Madeira is pleasant at any season. Even in winter the temperatures only reach those of Central Europe in the higher altitudes, while in Funchal they never fall below 18°C/64°F.

Madeira is an all-year-round destination

Since Madeira is also a favourite holiday destination for the Portuguese it can get very crowded in summer. So, if possible, avoid visiting the islands at that time of year, especially for a beach holiday on Porto Santo.

A visit in the off-season from April to June or late September to early November has the advantage of seeing Madeira in spring when the flowers are in full bloom, or just before harvest in autumn, and the sun is not too hot for comfort.

Off-season

Young People's Accommodation

Youth Hostels
Madeira has no youth hostels as such, but travellers on a limited budget will find there is plenty of private accommodation.

The tourist office in Funchal (see Information) can provide a list of cheap private accommodation where young people will also be welcome.

Pousadas
Madeira has two Government-run pousadas where walkers can find reasonably priced accommodation. During the holiday season it is necessary to book early:
 Pousada do Pico do Arieiro (on Pico do Arieiro); tel. 23 01 10
 Pousada dos Vinháticos (in Santo da Água); tel. 95 21 48

Camping
See entry

Index

Index

The Principal Places of Tourist Interest at a Glance

A map of the Island showing places of tourist interest at the end of the book

N.B.: The places listed above are merely a selection of the principal places of interest in themselves, or for attractions in the surrounding area. There are of course innumerable other places worth visiting, which have been highlighted by one or more stars.

Imprint

106 illustrations, 8 maps and plans, 1 large map at end of book

German text: Monika I. Baumgarten, Dr Peter H. Baumgarten, Heiner F. Gstaltmayr
Editorial work: die textwerkstatt (Heiner F. Gstaltmayr), Pfullingen
General direction: Rainer Eisenschmid, Baedeker Ostfildern
Cartography: Franz Huber, Munich; Franz Kaiser, Sindelfingen; Mairs Geographischer Verlag GmbH & Co., Ostfildern (large map)

Source of illustrations: Baedeker-Archiv (2); Dahle (6); Gstaltmayr (90); Museu de Arte Sacra, Funchal (2); Reid's Hotel (4); Ullstein Bilderdienst (3); ZEFA (1).

Editorial work: Margaret Court
English translation: Brenda Ferris, Crispin Warren

1st English edition 1997
Reprinted 2000

© Baedeker Stuttgart
Original German edition 1997

© Automobile Association Developments Limited 2000
English language edition worldwide

Published by AA Publishing (a trading name of Automobile Association Developments Limited, whose registered office is Norfolk House, Priestley Road, Basingstoke, Hampshire RG24 9NY; registered number 1878835).

Distributed in the United States and Canada by:
Fodor's Travel Publications, Inc.
201 East 50th Street
New York, NY 10022

A CIP catalogue record of this book is available from the British Library.

Licensed user: Mairs Geographischer Verlag GmbH & Co., Ostfildern

Printed in Italy by G. Canale & C. S.p.A., Turin

ISBN 0 7495 1733 6

Tourist highlights on Madeira

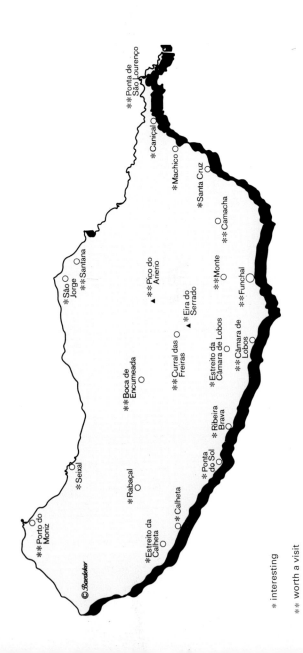

Ponta de São Lourenço **
Caniçal *
Machico *
Santa Cruz *
Camacha **
Santana **
São Jorge *
Pico do Arieiro **
Eira do Serrado *
Monte **
Funchal **
Boca de Encumeada **
Curral das Freiras **
Estreito da Câmara de Lobos *
Câmara de Lobos **
Seixal *
Ribeira Brava *
Rabaçal *
Ponta do Sol *
Porto do Moniz **
Calheta *
Estreito da Calheta *

© Baedeker

* interesting

** worth a visit